Robert E. Fogal
Ohio Presbyterian Retirement Services Foundation;
formerly of the Indiana University Center on Philanthropy
EDITOR-IN-CHIEF

FUNDRAISING MATTERS

TRUE STORIES OF HOW RAISING FUNDS FULFILLS DREAMS

Michael Seltzer
The Conservation Company
EDITOR

NUMBER 1, FALL 1993

FUNDRAISING MATTERS:
TRUE STORIES OF HOW RAISING FUNDS FULFILLS DREAMS
Michael Seltzer (ed.)
New Directions for Philanthropic Fundraising, No. 1, Fall 1993
Robert E. Fogal, Editor-in-Chief

Microfilm copies of issues and articles are available in 16 mm and 35 mm, as well as microfiche in 105 mm, through University Microfilms Inc., 300 North Zeeb Road, Ann Arbor, Michigan 48106-1346.

ISSN 1072-172X   ISBN 1-55542-715-4

NEW DIRECTIONS FOR PHILANTHROPIC FUNDRAISING is part of The Jossey-Bass Nonprofit Sector Series and is published quarterly by Jossey-Bass Inc., Publishers, 350 Sansome Street, San Francisco, California 94104-1310.

SUBSCRIPTIONS: Please see Ordering Information at back of book.

EDITORIAL CORRESPONDENCE should be sent to Robert E. Fogal, Ohio Presbyterian Retirement Services Foundation, OMNI Plaza, 4502 Darrow Rd., Rte. 91, Stow, OH 44224-1887.

Manufactured in the United States of America. Nearly all Jossey-Bass books, jackets, and periodicals are printed on recycled paper that contains at least 50 percent recycled waste, including 10 percent postconsumer waste. Many of our materials are also printed with vegetable-based ink; during the printing process these inks emit fewer volatile organic compounds (VOCs) than petroleum-based inks. VOCs contribute to the formation of smog.

Contents

Philanthropic Fundraising

VOLUNTARY GIVING is increasingly important to the work of non-profit organizations and to their philanthropic identity. Giving is also essential to the philanthropic tradition of voluntary action that achieves common good. Fundraising serves as a vehicle to encourage generosity, meet certain needs of nonprofit organizations and institutions, and provide opportunities to participate in building and sustaining the community good.

Much of what is available to read about fundraising is a journalistic treatment of one topic or another. This writing focuses mostly on fundraising techniques, which many perceive as prescriptions to guarantee results from fundraising efforts. More literature is needed to enhance the development of professionalism in the field by addressing important issues and concerns in fundraising philosophy and management.

New Directions for Philanthropic Fundraising aims to strengthen voluntary giving and build professionalism in fundraising by addressing how the concepts and traditions of philanthropy pertain to fundraising practice. In each quarterly volume of the series, authors will address practical themes in the context of the values of voluntarism and public benefit that characterize philanthropic organizations. Writers will approach fundraising as a multidimensional activity that is rooted in culture and society, builds human community, and provides individual fulfillment for the donor and the asker.

Examples of themes that will be analyzed and discussed include

Professionalism in fundraising

Education and training for fundraising

Preparing the organization for fundraising

Trusteeship and fundraising

NEW DIRECTIONS FOR PHILANTHROPIC FUNDRAISING, NO. 1, FALL 1993 © JOSSEY-BASS PUBLISHERS

Stewardship and accountability

Information management for fundraising

Voluntary service and voluntary giving

Major donors and gift planning

Capital campaigns and endowment building

Fundraising economics

Financial planning and management for fundraising

Cultural diversity in fundraising

Women and philanthropy

Grantmakers and fundraisers

Charity, philanthropy, and voluntary giving

Ethics and morality in fundraising.

Good books about fundraising stimulate us to reflect on what we do and why we do it; they should help us do what we do better. *New Directions for Philanthropic Fundraising* is designed to contribute to conversation and discourse among those who are interested in the philanthropic acquisition and use of money: fundraising managers, chief executive officers, volunteer leaders, other nonprofit staff, management assistance and fundraising consultants, fundraising educators, and grantmakers—all who want to think about fundraising practice as a critical dimension of voluntary action for the public good.

Robert E. Fogal
Editor-in-Chief
Ohio Presbyterian Retirement Services Foundation

Editor's Notes

OVER TWENTY-FIVE YEARS AGO, when I was a sophomore at an upstate New York university, a flyer on my dormitory bulletin board caught my eye. Its headline was "Do You Want to Go to Africa for the Summer?" All interested were invited to a meeting at the campus chapel.

My interest was piqued. I had only stepped foot out of the United States once, when I was thirteen, to accompany my father on a trip to Europe. Throughout my childhood, my father regularly took me to the Bronx Zoo on weekends, where I developed a strong love of animals. So a trip to Africa immediately caught my fancy. After all, I would be able to see wild animals in their natural habitats.

At the sparsely attended meeting, I was introduced to Operation Crossroads Africa, which sent teams of American and Canadian college students to African nations each summer to build cultural understanding between Africa and North America. Their program was touted as a precursor to the Peace Corps. As a past Crossroader from my university spoke about her summer in Senegal, I got swept up in the excitement filling the room. Then, she explained that the cost for the ten-week program was "only" $1,800. My enthusiasm dissipated rapidly. Sensing a change of mood in the audience, she quickly added that she raised the funds on her own, and that each of us could do the same. And so three prospective Crossroaders from my university spoke at meetings of every civic organization that we could find to solicit contributions. In return, we promised upon our return a slide presentation and talk on our summer experience. Thus, my career in fundraising began.

I recount this story simply to illustrate the connection between raising funds and fulfilling one's dreams. While I did not see as many wild

NEW DIRECTIONS FOR PHILANTHROPIC FUNDRAISING, NO. 1, FALL 1993 © JOSSEY-BASS PUBLISHERS

animals in Cameroon, West Africa, as I would have normally seen on one afternoon at a zoo in New York City, that summer was a pivotal experience of my life. Daily involvement with a people, a country, and a continent so different from my own enriched my life far more than I could have imagined. Most important, my sense of social justice was born.

Each year, people around the globe create new nonprofit organizations to address particular issues or concerns that they usually have confronted in their own lives. They set out to do "good work," to make a contribution to the quality of life of neighborhoods, communities, nations, and the world.

Americans have a special knack for birthing such organizations. In the 1980s, more than 193,000 nonprofits were created. Today, close to 1 million nonprofit organizations exist in the United States. Their individual annual budgets average less than $50,000. Collectively, they comprise 6.8 percent of the gross domestic product of the United States.

To sustain their efforts, nonprofits reach out to the general public—through bake sales, raffles, walkathons, direct mail, and other special events, and by just asking. In response, approximately 86 percent of all Americans give on average 2 percent of their incomes to charitable causes each year.

How do these organizations develop and flourish? The authors in this volume, "Fundraising Matters," recount the stories of eight organizations that were created during the last several decades. Some of the authors know their organizations intimately from the vantage point of executive director, founding board member, trainer, or consultant. Others are noted scholars and writers in the nonprofit field. Their intimate knowledge of the eight organizations and their familiarity with the vagaries of nonprofit management and fundraising provide the reader with a rare glimpse at the reasons behind the organizations' successes.

In Chapter One, Jennifer Leonard tells the story of the Neighborhood Film/Video Project of Philadelphia's International House and the project's founder, Linda Blackaby. Blackaby learned about grant seeking and foundations to give life to her vision of a new kind of media arts center, bringing the powerful medium of film to poor and minority neighborhoods, and, finally, to all Philadelphians. The collaboration between the project and the larger International House also illustrates how all good ideas do not necessarily need to lead to new organizations. For seventeen years, the project has flourished under the aegis of larger nonprofit institutions that have provided a strong underpinning for its work.

Max Martínez, in Chapter Two, captures the highlights of the evolution of the Guadalupe Cultural Arts Center, in San Antonio, Texas, into a major Latino arts institution. The center's story reveals the kinds of tensions that frequently accompany government support, and the role of private support for such institutions.

Kim Klein, in Chapter Three, brings to life the people behind Save Our Cumberland Mountains (SOCM) of east Tennessee. Working in an economically impoverished corner of Appalachia, SOCM's leaders managed to win impressive environmental and economic development victories, while raising significant sums from their constituents to finance their work.

In Chapter Four, Emmett D. Carson shares with us the saga of the National Black United Fund. Its founders, led by Walter Bremond, seized on the notion of creating a "systematic process or mechanism through which to financially support their own institutions" as a prerequisite of black empowerment. Their vision would ultimately lead to the development of fifteen independent fundraising organizations throughout the United States. These local black United Funds successfully undertook workplace solicitation campaigns, trailblazing this technique for many others.

Ronald Austin Wells, in Chapter Five, recounts the evolution of the American Indian College Fund from an idea to an important higher education institution that raised $7 million from ten thousand donors in 1991. The description of their first lunch briefing for foundation officers is particularly noteworthy. The fund effectively capitalized on the media attention that has been accorded to American Indians in recent years.

Stephen Silha, in Chapter Six, tells the story of Bailey-Boushay House of Seattle, Washington. From the vantage point of a board member, he provides a firsthand account of the first skilled nursing facility and day health care program designed and built specifically for people living with AIDS. The principles integral to the success of their $7.8 million campaign are truly universal.

Joan Flanagan, in Chapter Seven, writes about the Horizon Hospice in Chicago, of which she was a founding board member. Its founder, Ada Addington of Chicago, was moved to action by a newly emerging philosophy of care for the terminally ill. In less than fifteen years, the hospice's annual budget has grown to $2 million, and an endowment of $555,000 is in place.

In Chapter Eight, Naomi Tropp recalls how The Julian Center, a small women's agency in the heartland of the United States, built up a base of financial support to counter the unrecognized epidemic of violence against women in their midst. Their Amish Country Market will inspire others to think creatively in choosing an annual special event to raise funds and supporters.

In Chapter Nine, I conclude with an overview of the lessons we can draw from these accounts of successful nonprofit endeavors. Persistence and dedication to the cause are central themes in this regard, as is the ability to mobilize human and financial resources.

In each of these cases, fundraising provided the resources to attain a vision. Like the majority of people involved in the nonprofit sector, the leaders and their colleagues profiled here found themselves in similar straits to that college sophomore who wanted to go to West Africa. They needed to learn how to raise money. In learning how to do so, they were able to create lasting institutions.

In life, many of us find that we are reinventing the proverbial wheel when we set out on our chosen, and sometimes unchosen, paths. This is as true in the nonprofit sector as anywhere else. The readers of this journal will be able to draw from these stories inspiration and a wealth of ideas that they can apply to their own organizational settings. I hope that this volume will aid today's and tomorrow's nonprofit leaders in their pursuits and thus make our world a little better for all of us and for future generations.

Michael Seltzer
Editor

MICHAEL SELTZER *is a senior consultant specializing in nonprofit institutions and philanthropy at The Conservation Company, New York City; executive director of Funders Concerned About AIDS; and president of the Nonprofit Management Association.*

This case study of a successful merger between a media arts center and a residence program for international students explores the decision-making process that led to merger and its subsequent impact on mission, operations, and fundraising.

1

The Neighborhood Film/Video Project: Early merger was ticket to success

Jennifer Leonard

SINCE 1975, Linda Blackaby's romance with the big screen has brought Philadelphia a cornucopia of international and independent cinema. As the guiding light behind the Neighborhood Film/Video Project of Philadelphia's International House, Blackaby has devoted herself to making accessible a wide range of culturally, aesthetically, and socially important media works ignored by commercial movie houses. She has also become a lifeline for Philadelphia's independent film and video artists.

Blackaby exemplifies the drive, tenacity, and singleness of purpose of many nonprofit entrepreneurs. These characteristics have stood her well in marketing and grantsmanship. But rather than dilute these strengths with the demands of institutional management—a Peter Principle ascent deadly to many founder personalities—she chose early on to run her project within another organization.

NEW DIRECTIONS FOR PHILANTHROPIC FUNDRAISING, NO. 1, FALL 1993 © JOSSEY-BASS PUBLISHERS

The successful merger of Blackaby's original Neighborhood Film Project (renamed the Neighborhood Film/Video Project) and the International House of Philadelphia offers a model for dynamic, long-lasting coexistence built on trust, commitment, and mutual interest. The collaboration faced challenges in reconciling competing identities and creating a marketable mission from the unlikely merger of a media arts program with a center for international students. But by working through these problems together, each has come to enjoy both programmatic and fundraising success.

Finding a community need to fill

Blackaby came to Philadelphia in 1972, a former film society activist from the University of Oregon who helped finance her own graduate assistantship in English with movie screenings. A regular at Philadelphia screening rooms and film series, she soon came to the attention of Ralph Moore, an Episcopal minister who also exhibited art films. Moore took her on as a film festival volunteer and then made her manager of his Academy Screening Room (later to become the Roxy art film theater).

At that time, Philadelphia's nonprofit world used films chiefly for fundraising. Blackaby had raised antiwar funds that way. But her involvement in a festival of socially relevant films for the progressive Peoples' Fund (now Bread and Roses Community Fund) convinced her that more than money could be gained from movies: "It made more sense to me to show people films made by and about themselves, to do community education rather than raise money. Film could be used as a learning tool." In 1975, over coffee at a Chestnut Street eatery, she, Moore, and Michael Seltzer, then codirector of The Peoples' Fund, planned a center that would bring people to film, and film to the people.

The proposed center was designed to fill a crucial gap in Philadelphia's cultural arts offerings by exhibiting independent and international films that were not otherwise available to the city's audiences.

At the same time, the center would serve an educational role by hosting filmmaker workshops, providing a film reference service, and helping grass-roots groups use movies for educational and organizational purposes. For Seltzer, "The concept of the Neighborhood Film Project embraced the emerging media arts center trend around the country. It was a trailblazer in terms of where we were in independent film distribution and how films could be used in community education."

Starting with seed grants and ticket sales

To kick off the project, Blackaby submitted a grant proposal to the Philadelphia Foundation, which, like many community foundations, tended to be more receptive to new ventures than is characteristic of most private foundations and corporate donors. The Philadelphia Foundation was also known for its long-term support of community-based efforts, an even rarer characteristic among institutional funders. Its $11,000 seed grant to the project became the first of many grants this local funder provided over the years.

Blackaby had applied for the grant under the fiscal umbrella of the nonprofit Walnut Street Theatre, where Ralph Moore ran a film and video center. Then, unexpectedly, the Walnut Street Theatre withdrew from participation. In search of a screening facility—and the 501(c)(3) public charity status required to keep her first grant and seek others—Blackaby turned to the Christian Association of the University of Pennsylvania, where Moore wore his other hat as a man of God.

Originally a campus ministry, the Christian Association in the early 1970s resembled many of that era's ad hoc social incubators. It housed an eclectic group of progressive causes, from a women's art center and a "movement" print shop to a gay and lesbian counseling service. For the Neighborhood Film Project, it provided office space and part-time work for Blackaby, as well as the required 501(c)(3) status and use of an auditorium. With the Philadelphia

Foundation grant shifted to this new venue, the project was off and rolling.

Blackaby began bringing in community groups to preview films for grass-roots use. Maggie Kuhn and her Gray Panthers scrutinized films for evidence of ageism. The Lutheran Settlement House Women's Program screened works on women's lives to use in general equivalency diploma classes. Blackaby also took films out to the neighborhoods. The citywide Paul Robeson Festival brought films produced by African Americans and Latinos to seven community centers, as well as to the Philadelphia Museum of Art.

As Blackaby has recounted, "I had this idea that the people for whom the films are intended should look at them and evaluate them." Audience evaluations were filed for future reference. She then helped groups show chosen films to their constituencies, a task that involved lending equipment, teaching its use, and overseeing the acquisition of films from various distributors.

Two public film series helped draw attention to the project and produced critical earned income through ticket sales. The Real to Reel series offered new documentaries such as the Oscar-winning *Harlan County, U.S.A.* The International Cinema series screened modern masters such as Jean-Luc Godard and Lina Wertmuller. Both series featured meet-the-filmmaker events and background notes on each movie. All were eagerly consumed by a growing audience of local aficionados, who had few other opportunities to view noncommercial films in what was then the nation's fourth largest city.

Stretching resources and garnering grants

Due to the makeshift funding typical of many start-up nonprofits, project staff lived a hand-to-mouth existence for a long time. Blackaby and her codirector lived on unemployment for a year. They used university work-study students for cheap help; during the academic year, the project paid only 10 percent of the students' salaries, while government funds made up the balance. (Later, when the budget permitted, Blackaby hired the best of these temporary helpers for permanent staff.)

Technical assistance providers also helped the project stretch resources. A volunteer from Community Accountants set up the books for ongoing posting by a part-time bookkeeper. The Philadelphia Clearinghouse for Community Funding Resources, a management support organization cofounded by Seltzer, encouraged and guided Blackaby's natural gift for grant seeking.

"I am an obsessive proposal writer," recalls Blackaby. Her persistence paid off. She received more support from the Philadelphia Foundation and secured Pennsylvania Council on the Arts (PCA) grants for the two film series at the Christian Association. When the National Endowment for the Arts (NEA) balked at funding what appeared to be a university-based religious organization, she and colleagues took the project's film schedules to Washington, D.C., to ask again whether it was worth applying. NEA then said yes, and its peer review panels granted the project several thousands of dollars.

Blackaby applied in different NEA categories for exhibit money, for workshop money, for services to the field. NEA also helped fund publication of *IN FOCUS: A Guide to Using Films* (1980), a book for community organizations co-written by Blackaby, Dan Georgakas, and New York filmmaker Barbara Margolis *(On the Line; Are We Winning, Mommy?: America and the Cold War)*. Fundraising for the book brought Blackaby to the notice of New York and national funders.

During these early years, Blackaby consolidated what would continue to be the project's basic mix of funding: earned income from ticket sales, supplemented by foundation, state, and federal government grants. As the project budget approached that of the Christian Association, internal support began to wane. The Christian Association decided to refocus its mission on campus affairs rather than the larger community and dropped sponsorship of the international film series. Blackaby's project was forced to find another auditorium.

Surviving overexpansion at International House

The Quakers, who helped to settle Philadelphia, have long been advocates of international harmony and understanding. It was the City of Brotherly Love that gave birth to both the American Friends Service Committee and the Women's International League for Peace and Freedom. It also spawned International House of Philadelphia, the first American charity devoted to supporting international students and integrating them into university and city life.

Initially formed to soften culture shock and stem discrimination against foreign students, International House developed and maintained close ties to members of the community with international interests. This dual focus distinguishes the original International House, founded in 1910, from three later American International Houses founded with Rockefeller Foundation assistance at Columbia University, the University of Chicago, and the University of California at Berkeley. The central focus of these three houses is on campus life.

International House of Philadelphia's early social, cultural, and educational programs for international students gradually developed a residential component, which, beginning in 1959, enjoyed a promising trial run in a small downtown hotel leased for a dollar a year from the Quakers. When the city of Philadelphia moved to demolish the hotel as part of a road-widening project, the International House board decided to build its own residential and program center near the West Philadelphia campuses of the University of Pennsylvania and Drexel University. In 1970, with $5 million from the William Penn Foundation and backing from other local funders, a majestic fourteen-story concrete and glass structure arose on Chestnut Street adjacent to the University of Pennsylvania. Its award-winning architectural design featured soaring public galleries and suites of small bedrooms designed to encourage student mingling in spacious common rooms.

Unfortunately, the lofty building became a classic case of over-expansion. "They were very optimistic in 1970," wryly observes International House development director Theodora Ashmead. The galleries proved costly to heat and cool. Prospective residents rejected the tiny bedrooms and common areas, preferring larger study quarters and on-campus social spots.

The building never reached full occupancy. Its slim revenues were overwhelmed by operational costs and by repayment of a federal Housing and Urban Development (HUD) loan necessitated by con-struction overruns. Maintenance was deferred indefinitely. The bud-get deficits grew at such a rapid rate that, in 1974, an International House strategic planning meeting considered going out of business as one of its five options.

But the business people on the board, who have shared their wis-dom and worked hard at critical junctures through the years, decid-ed to recommit themselves to International House's future. They took steps to stem the hemorrhaging budget, paring back on pro-grams and making financial survival the only criterion in adminis-trative decisions.

Meeting mutual needs through merger

In July 1976, the International House president hired Ellen B. Davis as the new program director. Her assignment was to do whatever she could to create programs—without spending a dime. "When I came, International House had bottomed out. There were no programs. It was a wasteland, a fortress, uninhabited in terms of programs," says Davis. "We wanted to start the resident activities going again, and one area I was interested in was films. Somebody told me the best thing [in film] in Philadelphia was on the Penn campus. I didn't want to start anything going if it already existed."

Davis met Blackaby just as the Christian Association was withdrawing support from the international film festival and proposed that the two groups work together. International House would provide its multipurpose Hopkinson Hall for screenings, Blackaby would provide the films and program expertise

The setting was hardly luxurious. Blackaby personally hauled over the projectors for each showing at International House. The little lighting booth was so small that people joked about needing thin projectionists. The local *Welcomat* newspaper, which closely covers the art film scene, described the Hopkinson Hall chairs as "ass-killing." But, says Blackaby, "We had air conditioning! That was important." Davis adds, "At that point, it was a step up for all of us."

They agreed to split costs on the series, and International House took the chance of guaranteeing the local match for the PCA and NEA grants. Fortunately, ticket sales were strong. "We were doing premieres here of major films—in 16 millimeter," says Blackaby, smiling. The move was very popular with International House residents, who were delighted that the foreign films they had trudged several blocks to see at the Christian Association were now in their building. The film series adopted the marketing position, "See international films in the company of people to whom they are not foreign at all."

About the same time, another established program took up quarters at International House. Like Blackaby's project, the Folklife Center came complete with expertise—the preservation and exhibition of ethnic and folk art—and NEA funding. "It was great for us," recalls Davis, "because, with no cash outlay, we were doing things, literally just giving away space to bring in some energy, creativity, and things of value. We had the choice of starting at ground zero, or of tapping the strength of these existing programs."

While the project was offering the Real to Reel series and working with community groups through the Christian Association, Davis and Blackaby began discussing a merger. "I was never interested in doing programs just for Penn students, especially once I had made the decision to apply for public funding," says Blackaby, referring to the Christian Association's changing focus. "I had a responsibility to do things for the public. I also needed to move off the campus, which is a barrier to some people."

The trust between these two spinners of substance out of thin air—who to this day complete each other's sentences—led to a merger agreement effective July 1, 1979. The Real to Reel series was perhaps the touchiest element of the deal for the International House board. "We had to work it out so that we were presenting, but not advocating, points of view," says Davis.

Blackaby brought to the merger her project's popular programs, established funding, and growing national stature. International House provided office, storage, and exhibition space; a board and nonprofit status; and an administrative support structure that was sorely needed to assist the fast-growing project. "If the project hadn't moved over, it wouldn't have been able to manage much longer," says Blackaby.

The merger guaranteed Blackaby's freedom from other headaches as well. "I see other media arts centers struggling so over real estate. Let's face it, a movie theater is a big facility to manage. . . . Michael [Seltzer] was always trying to get me to form a board, but I resisted. I think I didn't ever want to become one of those one-person burnout cases who do their own bookkeeping and everything else," she notes.

Crafting a stronger postmerger mission

The collaboration worked. The Neighborhood Film Project thrived in its supportive new quarters. Its work drew widespread notice, and, in 1984, Pennsylvania Governor Richard Thornburgh awarded Blackaby the Hazlett Memorial Award for Excellence in the Arts. As part of International House's new "art center," together with the Folklife Center, the project also helped draw Philadelphians into the big building at 37th and Chestnut. Its audiences became potential patrons of the House's cafe and museum-quality craft store, potential supporters of the resident programs, and even potential volunteers. International House's image began to take on some needed polish.

From a financial point of view as well, the crisis was over. International House was now running small budget surpluses instead of deficits. Ellen Davis took over as president in 1981 with widespread support. Under her leadership, the board agreed to take stock of twelve years' worth of accumulated problems—and, in some cases, opportunities. A strategic planning process, begun in 1982, delineated these needs: complete refurbishment of the long-neglected building, including living quarters, common areas, and staff offices; conversion of Hopkinson Hall into a comfortable, modern screening facility; decoration and furnishing of the sterile galleria to stress internationalism, encourage foot traffic, and draw patrons for the cafe and museum store; expansion of services to international business travelers and to local groups seeking conference space; creation of a small student center; and computerization of office systems. The board also envisioned a modest endowment, income from which could cover the annual loan payment to HUD and smooth out fluctuations in revenue for the art center programs.

With the assistance of fundraising counsel Barnes & Roche, International House created a case statement showing $6.4 million in capital needs and embarked on a feasibility study. In June 1984, Barnes & Roche offered its advice: Start with a $1.7 million goal and see how it goes.

Based on its interviews, Barnes & Roche felt that International House had too few potential campaign leaders, too few major donors, too narrow an appeal, and too many low-priority needs. The firm suggested that International House spend the next two years raising what it could in a noncampaign mode, while broadening the annual membership and other prospective donor bases.

The report also disclosed that many International House board members and supporters failed to understand the mutually beneficial relationship between the art center programs and the traditional residential activities. For these interviewees, the "new" International House had a mission that just did not gel: "Over and over, interviewees commented on the importance of having better justification for the existence of the Neighborhood Film Project and the Folklife Center. While most acknowledged that these were programs of distinction, they also did not see them as embodying International House's basic mission. As we understand it, these programs in fact attract funds, particularly from the corporate sector, which would otherwise be unavailable to the House and give the house greater visibility in the community. It is this kind of justification which needs to be specifically delineated in the case for support" (Barnes & Roche, 1984).

The earliest written mission statement for International House stated, in 1965, that its purpose was "to contribute to the search for international understanding and peace" (International House of Philadelphia, 1988). By the time of the Barnes & Roche study in 1984, the mission of International House embraced domestic as well as international diversity: "to promote international and intercultural understanding." Faced with the feasibility study findings, the board, in 1984, decided on another revision that aggressively included the art center programs: "International House of Philadelphia, a residence, program, and cultural center, exists to promote international and intercultural understanding. A variety of programs serve this goal: providing a unique living experience for 400 residents from 51 countries; sponsoring nationally-recognized media arts and folklife programs; and offering services for foreign students throughout the Delaware Valley" (International House of Philadelphia, 1988).

Making the film project an asset in International House fundraising

Rather than being unrelated adjuncts of International House, the art programs thus moved into center stage as embodiments of the multicultural, multiethnic mission of International House. International House (1988) explained in its strategic plan that the arts represent "a powerful vehicle for international and intercultural exchange and understanding. . . . Both the Neighborhood Film Project and the Folklife Center sought to involve the public in the mission of International House, the Film Project through its presentation of international and independent films and videos that represent the diversity of creative and cultural views that shape our world today and the Folklife Center through its commitment to preserving and presenting diverse traditional ethnic and international cultures." The strategic plan also pointed out that the art center had brought nationally respected programs to the facility's underutilized space, which led to the involvement of the broader community and raised the House's attractiveness to both annual and capital funders.

In accordance with the Barnes & Roche recommendations, International House made the case for its expanded mission to its supporters. It added development staff, expanded its membership and donor bases, cultivated foundations and corporations, and created a vibrant public image as a multiprogram center for international understanding. Over the next four years, it raised not its restated goal of $1.7 million but $3 million in its Campaign for Renewal: "New funding sources such as the Kresge Foundation were intrigued with the unique and successful blend of programs that related to a mission that they respected. . . . Without the totality of programs, even the original goal of $1.7 million would probably not have been achieved" (International House of Philadelphia, 1988).

The funds allowed International House to renovate parts of its entire building, including the refurnishing of living quarters, the creation of a conference center facility that now yields earned income and a student center, and the modernization of many of the building's basic systems. A wealth of new signs includes folk-art-style ceramic donor plaques that decorate the concrete walls.

The arts programs proved to be critical in attracting overall support. A hefty $1 million of campaign proceeds, contributed by the Kresge Foundation, Pew Charitable Trusts, and the NEA, went to the renovation of Hopkinson Hall. All three of these funders helped International House raise additional funds by setting stringent matching requirements for their gifts.

"It's hard to imagine doing fundraising for International House without a program like the Neighborhood Film/Video Project," says development vice president Shirley Trauger, who is now directing the Campaign for Permanence, a fundraising project that primarily revisits some of the endowment goals set aside in 1984. In turn, International House's sophisticated fundraising operation has given some relief to Blackaby, who until recently continued to do most of the project's proposal writing. Now a computer plays an essential role. "That was the last piece to be institutionalized," Blackaby says.

Presenting a unified public image

Programmatically, the Neighborhood Film/Video Project and International House are flying high. They have produced seminal festivals of Algerian, Asian, Iranian, Latin American, and animated films. The Philadelphia Independent Film and Video Association, which Blackaby founded when the project merged with International House, now serves three hundred local media artists with workshops, peer screenings, newsletters, and referrals.

In the spring of 1992, International House conducted its first annual Philadelphia Festival of World Cinema, a forty-film, thirteen-venue extravaganza organized by the Neighborhood Film/Video Project. It drew rave reviews in the press and inspired one local theater owner, Posel, to describe Blackaby as "Philadelphia's most precious film resource" (Rickey, 1992). The festival also illustrated one last vestige of the complications of merger—names.

While International House and Ellen Davis have been remarkable in allowing, even encouraging, a prominent local and national identity for the Neighborhood Film/Video Project, they are also careful to position it as a distinguished *part* of International House. When the Philadelphia Festival of World Cinema was proposed, all agreed on the importance of using a citywide name for the new festival and of giving prominent billing to International House, not to the Neighborhood Film/Video Project, as its producer. Inside the printed programs, Blackaby has her say as festival director, alongside welcomes from the mayor and from the chair and president of International House.

Blackaby does not begrudge the give and take. She knows that she benefits from an institutional structure that gives her the freedom to be, well, uninstitutional. She describes today's Neighborhood Film/Video Project as "right out there on the margins of Philadelphia's cultural environment, where we're supposed to be. It's not financially feasible for the Ritz to mount 'Ten Years of Algerian Cinema,' but it's perfect for us."

According to Blackaby, International House board members have suggested that she change the name of the project, saying it sounds too provisional. "Well, it *is* provisional. Besides," says Blackaby, sweeping her hand at the fourteen stories of windows rising above her, "they already have International House. Isn't that magnificent enough?" Indeed it is—thanks, in part, to the Neighborhood Film/Video Project.

References

Barnes & Roche. *Feasibility Study Report for International House of Philadelphia.* Philadelphia: Barnes & Roche, 1984.

Blackaby, L., Georgakas, D., and Margolis, B. *IN FOCUS: A Guide to Using Films.* New York: New York Zoetrope, 1980.

International House of Philadelphia. *Five-Year Plan: 1989–1993.* Philadelphia: International House, 1988.

Rickey, C. "Birth of a Film Festival." *Philadelphia Inquirer,* Mar. 15, 1992, p. N1.

JENNIFER LEONARD *is president and executive director of the Rochester Area Foundation in New York. Her articles about charity and philanthropy have appeared in the* Los Angeles Times, Columbia Journalism Review, *and* Foundation News.

*A small, nonprofit Latino arts and cultural orga-
nization faces a series of critical decisions regarding
a diversification of funding sources and a reassessment
of its artistic mission to create a balance between the
needs of the local community and those of the larger, more diverse Latino community in the United
States.*

2

Guadalupe Cultural Arts Center:
A community arts success

Max Martínez

NONPROFIT ORGANIZATIONS, if they are to survive and achieve
even a modest degree of success, must develop a diverse range of
funding sources. At the time of its founding in 1979, the Guadalupe
Cultural Arts Center (GCAC), in San Antonio, Texas, depended
almost entirely on a single source of funding. The city of San Antonio provided nearly 95 percent of GCAC revenues. Furthermore, as
an agency existing solely on municipal largesse, there were expectations placed on GCAC that had less to do with the arts than with
political and social considerations. GCAC would not become a genuine arts and cultural institution until it moved into the forefront
of the Latino arts, where it could attract funding from sources associated with arts and cultural giving.

NEW DIRECTIONS FOR PHILANTHROPIC FUNDRAISING, NO. 1, FALL 1993 © JOSSEY-BASS PUBLISHERS

Latinos begin to acquire political power

Before 1979, there were but three arts and cultural institutions that received support, albeit it minimal, from the city of San Antonio. None of the three institutions (San Antonio Symphony, San Antonio Museum Association, and San Antonio Little Theater) was the least responsive to the Latino community, which was over half of the city's population. In fact, the entire political, social, and economic structure of the city failed to recognize the Latino population.

Several years prior to 1979, the city had entered into an agreement with the U.S. Department of Justice to change the method of electing municipal representatives from an at-large system to single-member districts. At that time, the city council was working out the kinks in the new political system. Latinos held a majority of seats on the council, but there was a transitional period in progress. No one as yet could tell what that majority meant to the city in general and to Latinos in particular. San Antonio was and remains a relatively poor city. The arts had previously not been a priority for the city council, and it was unlikely that the new council would change that. There were more pressing projects and needs within the underserved Latino community to be met.

San Antonio, however, has had a long and thriving artistic tradition among Latinos. Only a relative handful of artists had ever formally organized. They relied principally on the Mexican tradition of the *Tertulia*, which is a group of writers and other artists who meet to exchange ideas and talk about their work. In San Antonio, there were such groups of literary people, visual artists, and community action groups with a strong link to the arts.

In the Chicano movement, beginning in the early 1970s, the arts were used as an instrument of social change. Poets and visual artists imbued their works with strong social messages. Theatrical works were employed to dramatize the social conditions in which Latinos suffered. It was not uncommon, for example, for a political rally to begin with a musical presentation, a poetry reading, and a theater skit. San Antonio was fortunate to have a growing number of artists working independently yet prepared to participate in a more formal and organized manner.

In 1979, there were several arts groups, new to the municipal budget in the prior year or two, that again applied for modest grants from the city. The city manager, faced with a tight budget, recommended that no Latino arts group receive funding for the 1979–1980 fiscal year. When pressed to explain the basis for his decision, the city manager bluntly stated that the Latino arts "did not measure up to the symphony and the museum." On the surface, these comments were volatile in the extreme and had the potential to polarize the community along racial and ethnic lines. This blunder cost the city manager his job and, in the end, led to increased funding for Latino arts.

Latino arts groups organize

As a result of rallies, demonstrations, and discussions among artists and community leaders, a consortium of Latino arts groups was established in 1979. The precursor to GCAC, the Performance Artists Nucleus (PAN), was selected as the administrative agent for the consortium due to its designation by the Internal Revenue Service as a nonprofit, tax-exempt agency.

Although the program year began with high hopes, the difficulties of the arrangement soon became evident. Foremost, each member group of the consortium had its own board of directors, its own staff, and its own programming mission. None of the groups had been in existence for more than a year or two, and thus all were neophytes in administrative and fiscal management. The chief responsibility of PAN was to ensure strict compliance with municipal regulations regarding city funds. As PAN struggled to maintain compliance with these regulations, the member groups of the consortium interpreted its actions as assaults on their independence.

The consortium was doomed to failure. At the same time, the San Antonio City Council had moved forward with arts funding, appropriating nearly $3 million in the 1981–1982 fiscal year. The lion's share of this appropriation was earmarked for the museum, symphony, and PAN. PAN, in fact, was slated for an increase of 100 percent, amounting to nearly $500,000. This appropriation of funds occurred as the consortium was crumbling, the result of territorial disputes and internecine squabbling. In order to justify continued funding, it was evident that the consortium would have to be streamlined and placed on a firm administrative and financial footing.

A single organization is established

In its incorporation papers with the state of Texas, PAN's mission was the preservation, presentation, promotion, and development of Mexican American arts. PAN had served its mission principally through its work as an umbrella for the consortium. With the concurrence of the city council, the leadership of PAN, primarily the board of directors, met in October 1982 and approved a shift from an administrative unit to an operational agency that presented and developed its own programming.

To reflect its renewed dedication to the arts and cultural life of the city, the PAN Board of Directors voted to change the name of the organization to the Guadalupe Cultural Arts Center. Two group members of the disbanded consortium agreed to become operating programs within GCAC. These became the Xicano Music Program and the Visual Arts Program. The Literature and Theater Arts programs were also formally established at this meeting. Underlying the changes was the belief that GCAC would become a genuine arts and cultural institution. However, it would take three years before GCAC was firmly on the road to stability.

Search for professional management

The board of directors recognized that city funding of the organization, as a single source of support, was fragile at best and would depend largely on annual lobbying efforts before the city council. The board also recognized that they needed to appoint a professional staff to give substance to its operational mission. At the behest of a city council member, who was then a major supporter of GCAC, a close political ally of his campaign manager was appointed as executive director. This individual turned out to be less than qualified, and she was removed from the position within six months. The board of directors, sensitive to the need for professional management, instituted a nationwide search for an executive director in an effort to remove the organization from the limitations imposed by local politics.

While there was an upheaval at the very top of the organization, the staff continued to build on the strengths of their separate programs. There was an array of classes in music, visual arts, literature, and drama. The Tejano Conjunto Festival, which had been inaugurated in 1981, attracted a major sponsor in a local corporation. GCAC received its first National Endowment for the Arts (NEA) grant from Expansion Arts. The Literature Program followed with a NEA grant in 1982. Applications were submitted to the Texas Commission on the Arts. The potential of GCAC to become a major institution was evident. For example, the San Antonio CineFestival, which at the time had been in existence for six years and which was then the only film festival by and about Latinos in the nation, was transferred to GCAC for management and operations. Along with the film festival, GCAC received two grants from national foundations.

The removal of the executive director made for a fractious spring and summer of 1983. As the turbulence subsided at GCAC, the search to fill the position of executive director began in earnest. The board of directors set the procedure by which a committee reviewed the applicant pool and selected without prejudice those qualified for the position. From this list, three candidates were to be invited for formal interviews. This procedure had been agreed to by unanimous vote just a few months earlier; however, there were divisions on the board of directors that were about to erupt and bring yet another crisis to GCAC.

Pork barrel versus artistic management

Funding for Latino arts had been won by the unity and passion of the entire Latino community. Artists and political and community activists had banded together to form a united front with which to demand an equitable distribution of municipal funds for arts. Once the city budget included funding for Latino arts, a strong sentiment emerged among a few self-interested people that those artists who had been a part of the struggle to obtain the funding deserved the reward of jobs and support. There was an expectation that only residents of San Antonio would be eligible for the jobs.

From the standpoint of some board members, GCAC was a local community organization and, as such, ought to be managed by local people, with a focus directed solely to the support of local artists. The six-member board was evenly divided between those who saw GCAC as an organization with national implications and those who saw the organization as an opportunity to support local artists. The two views were not necessarily incompatible; however, as many of the applicants for executive director presented credentials that far outstripped those of any local applicant, it became evident that the position would be filled by someone who had not been part of the struggle to obtain Latino funding from the city.

The same city council member whose political ally had so badly served the agency stepped into this volatile mixture. He had been instrumental in convincing his colleagues on the city council to fund Latino arts. He assumed that any Latino organization that received city funding owed a special allegiance to him personally, and he expected Latinos arts groups to consult with him on all of their programming and administrative decisions. Three GCAC board members met with this council member to request his intervention in the appointment of an executive director for GCAC. These board members felt that the appointment of an outsider would result in the abandonment of support for local artists. Furthermore, they believed that an outsider might not respect the efforts of local activists and, indeed, might take the organization in a direction that would undermine their own influence.

Although the search committee of the board had settled on the candidates to be formally interviewed, one more individual was added to the list of finalists at the request of the council member through his appointed member on the board. The three board members allied with the council member called, first, to overturn the selection procedures that previously had been unanimously approved and, second, to present a motion to appoint the council member's candidate, without interviews of other candidates and without further discussion. This attempt to wrest control of the organization failed, however, as the vote was deadlocked and the motion was tabled. This parliamentary defeat proved to be the last time anything but professional and artistic concerns played a part in the internal decisions of GCAC.

Professional management assumes leadership

Pedro A. Rodríguez, a native of San Antonio, with graduate degrees in the fine arts, presented an impressive history of administrative positions in his application for the executive director position at GCAC. He was director of Arts and Cultural Affairs for the city of Austin, Texas. No other candidate came even close to Rodríguez's qualifications. He was appointed executive director in October 1983 and was permitted three months to establish a smooth transition from his job in Austin to GCAC. In the interim, he spent two days a week in San Antonio, familiarizing himself with GCAC.

Even before he assumed his full-time duties in January 1984, Rodríguez had a daunting task before him. The operational year had begun in October. The program departments continued with their scheduled offerings. However, the Literature and Theater Arts programs were without directors and essentially dormant. Construction had begun to refurbish the Guadalupe Theater, which, when completed, would be managed by GCAC. A manager and technical personnel would have to be appointed.

Next, and equally as pressing, was the task of reestablishing vital links to the community, whose support was crucial to GCAC's continued existence. The appointment of Rodríguez caused an intense reaction from a small number of people in the community. Rodríguez immediately set about mending fences and providing assurances that his administration would not ignore local artists and that his intention was to build a cultural arts center actively involved in the community. It was possible, he reasoned, to serve the needs of the community at the same time that GCAC attempted to fulfill its potential as a Latino arts organization with a nationwide impact. Nothing and no one need be sacrificed in the pursuit of both goals.

In his assessment of the internal condition of GCAC at the time of his appointment, Rodríguez saw several problem areas. Some of them could be easily solved by administrative fiat. Others required delicate guidance, firm leadership, and careful persuasion.

Redefining the character of the board of directors

A major area of concern was the board of directors. On what can be called the progressive side of the board, there were a civil rights attorney, an artist, and a university professor. On the other side were an insurance company employee, a labor organizer, and a drug abuse program director. In the best of circumstances, this was a board representative of the Latino community, even if the ratio of male to female, which stood at four to two, could be improved.

The difficulties on the board of directors were owing to the nature of the organization itself. There had never before been a Latino institution of such size and mission. There was no practical experience to be had anywhere to serve as a model of operations. The chair of the board understood this and made a conscious effort to permit the organization to proceed according to its own momentum. He was opposed to the board involving itself in the internal workings of

GCAC. More than anyone, the chair understood that in an organization as unique as GCAC, the best way to proceed was through trial and error. There were bound to be mistakes, waste, and mismanagement. However, in the long run, the organization would settle into its strengths. What GCAC needed was time.

Broadening the scope of the organization

Another immediate problem that Rodríguez faced was the structure of the organization. The organization had come into existence as a patchwork of separate groups. Two of the existing programs had had separate identities prior to their incorporation into GCAC. In many ways, they continued to operate as independent units, with little regard for the unity of the entire organization. As the new program directors were installed, they took their lead from the other programs and sought to operate independently as well. Rodríguez set out to meld the programs into one organization. This task of program integration was not just a matter of subordinating the programs to a central executive unit. The issues were at once parochial and international, and, at the level of aesthetics, they called for an examination of the arts in the Latino community.

Three of GCAC's festivals illustrate the range and complexity of the GCAC. The oldest, CineFestival, had been founded to feature the works of Mexican American filmmakers and, to a lesser extent, works about Mexican Americans. The newly appointed Guadalupe Theater manager and director of CineFestival recognized that the festival could not be sustained with purely Mexican American works. He expanded the scope of the festival to include films from Latin America and works by and about Latinos other than Chicanos. The Tejano Conjunto Festival was limited to the music of Mexican Americans. Conjunto is an accordion-based music that originated in the borderlands between Mexico and Texas and is considered a unique Mexican American contribution to music. The third festival, the San Antonio BookFair, displays the literary works of small and independent presses, with a strong emphasis on the works of Mexican Americans.

GCAC was faced with the need to reinterpret its programming and still remain within its mission to present, preserve, develop, and promote Latino arts. The classes of arts instruction offered by all of the GCAC programs were exemplary in serving the needs of the community. Tuition was kept low, and instruction sites were located throughout the community. In the Music Program, for example, instruments were provided to students who could not afford to rent or buy them. None of GCAC's festivals and programs was presented outside of the organization's primary mission. If anything, the festivals proved that an inclusive approach was preferable to a narrow interpretation calling strictly for the work of Mexican Americans. (It should be noted that the cultural diversity in GCAC's programming was in existence a good five years before it became a matter of urgent national concern.)

Unifying the mission of the organization as a fundraising strategy

The matter of GCAC revenues was also troubling. Only 10 percent came from grants, contributions, and earned income, with city funding accounting for the remainder. GCAC would not long survive unless its funding base was greatly expanded. Here again was the problem of the organization unsure of its identity, waxing between a direction toward a national constituency and the call for a more local focus in its programs. Funding from national foundations and corporations depended on the former orientation. In the latter, GCAC would require intensive funding from local businesses and corporations. The latter choice was untenable. Yet, the two would have to be reconciled to the satisfaction of GCAC's local constituency and in such a way as to make GCAC attractive as a funding recipient for national donors.

As Pedro Rodríguez settled into his day-to-day activities at GCAC, attending meetings and devising strategies to place GCAC on sound administrative, artistic, and financial bases, the city council member who had done the most to fund GCAC became actively involved in an attempt to dismantle the organization. In 1984, the question of national versus local orientation came to a head. Ultimately, the issues involved had little to do with the arts. At stake was control of the organization.

The central issue concerned the nature of Latino art and the coming changes in the Latino community. On one side, there was an insistence that GCAC promote the art of Mexican Americans as it had served the political and social activities of the Chicano movement. The focus of the movement itself had already split into more attenuated activity. At the same time, a national Latino constituency was on the rise. GCAC was already positioning itself to become a center with a national influence and thus through its programming could establish the forceful presence of Mexican Americans at a national level. Instead of reacting to the arts as they became available, GCAC's board and staff aimed to move ahead of the arts and become an institution on the cutting edge of the Latino arts.

This ambition was difficult to communicate to people who basically perceived the arts as entertainment. They were amused by friends who were poets and musicians and by visual artists who recycled images and icons long after they had served their usefulness in the Chicano movement. GCAC's staff tended to support artists who demonstrated genuine talent and world-class creativity while maintaining relevance to the local community. It was art of the highest standards firmly grounded in Chicano aesthetics. If the local activists could exert little or no control over the direction of GCAC, even more difficult for them to accept was the world-class creativity of the art and artists presented.

If the struggle in February 1984 was over control of the organization, it was as much a struggle over the nature of Latino art. There followed a harrowing six months of accusations, charges, and political maneuvering that tested the mettle of the GCAC board, staff, and supporters in the community. To the credit of the GCAC staff, none of the programming was affected. GCAC continued with its full schedule of events, even if none of the program directors could be sure from one day to the next whether he or she would even have a job for much longer. In the end, the council member and his cohorts lost their bid to deny funding to GCAC. In fact, on the positive side, the city council took arts funding out of the political arena and placed it in the hands of a committee of peers in the arts. The committee would recommend to the city council the arts groups deserving of city funding.

Almost immediately, when the Arts and Cultural Committee convened to evaluate applications for city funding, GCAC was faced with another, but this time more manageable crisis. The difficulty concerned the proportion of city funding needed relative to the overall budget of GCAC. In seeking a higher proportion of city funding, GCAC argued that the organization was relatively new and that given the opportunity, GCAC would make an outstanding return on the city's investment.

Professional development and aggressive fundraising as a function of board and staff

In the interim of the city budget process, Rodríguez hired a director of development, who set in motion a major effort to raise money for GCAC. Central to these efforts was the strategy to raise funds from a diverse range of sources. Because of its multidisciplinary configuration, GCAC was eligible for a number of grants from the NEA. The Texas Commission for the Arts provided organizational support, and grants were awarded for specific projects. Where possible, a humanities component was added to projects in order to educate the public and to qualify for funding from the Texas Committee for the Humanities. Applications and proposals were submitted to national foundations and corporations. At the same time, with the assistance of board members and community leaders, local business and corporations began to respond favorably to GCAC's fundraising efforts.

By 1986, there had been immense progress in the organization. The board of directors had been expanded and reformed. The new board members were responsive to the organization and not to any outside agenda from a concealed constituency. Greater emphasis was placed on the fundraising duties of board members. There was considerable progress made among the program directors, who settled into a genuinely unified organization.

The crowning achievement of GCAC during its first decade was an application to the NEA Challenge Grant Program. The grant, although small by NEA Challenge standards, was of symbolic importance to GCAC. The successful application was uniformly supported by a cross section of community leaders, including Henry Cisneros, then mayor of San Antonio, and Congressman Henry B. Gonzales. The board of directors was invigorated by the prospect of meeting the terms of the grant.

Although it took considerable effort and inordinate patience from all concerned, GCAC managed to complete its first decade of operations in an exemplary manner. For an organization that began with 95 percent city funding, that figure had been reduced to 32 percent in 1990. Earned income had risen to account for another third of revenues. The remaining revenue came from national foundations and corporations, such as Rockefeller and Ford, and Anheuser-Busch. A plaque commemorating ten years of programs and services to the community was dedicated in 1991 by the president of the Republic of Mexico.

According to Pedro Rodríguez, the first decade proved to city administrators and the community that GCAC is an important part of the cultural life of the city. The investment in its development has been returned tenfold. GCAC has a national and international reputation. In fact, GCAC serves as a model for Latino and other organizations of color throughout the nation. The staff members are in constant demand to consult and advise on the establishment of similar centers. They also are active participants on the boards of national organizations.

While it took virtually an entire decade to establish its administrative, artistic, and financial stability, GCAC is presently at another crossroads. Although the organization has made tremendous strides in diversifying and increasing its revenues, the national fundraising picture is bleak. In order to maintain its present levels of funding and to increase revenues necessary to proceed with expansion and new programs, GCAC must become more aggressive in its fundraising strategies. A professional fundraising consultant has developed a computer program designed to assist GCAC in its fundraising. All of the elements necessary to carry GCAC to the completion of its second decade are in place.

MAX MARTÍNEZ *is a writer and staff member of the Guadalupe Cultural Arts Center, San Antonio, Texas.*

Today, in the eighteen counties of east Tennessee in Appalachia, more than thirteen hundred families belong to a unique grass-roots community organization called Save Our Cumberland Mountains (SOCM). For twenty years, SOCM has worked to improve the quality of life of its members and their communities by finding solutions to specific local problems. This chapter recounts how a membership-based group situated in the coalfields of Appalachia now raises $250,000 each year to support its work.

3

Save Our Cumberland Mountains

Kim Klein

Never doubt that a small group of thoughtful, committed citizens can change the world; indeed, it's the only thing that ever has.

—MARGARET MEAD

IN THE SUMMERTIME, the soft green hills are covered in a light gray haze that is a mixture of fog and mist, and the basis of the name Smoky Mountains. If observers look closely, they will see that the green is not one color but rather dozens of shades, reflecting the ecology of the Appalachian mountain chain, which has more kinds of trees than anywhere but the Amazon Basin. Adding to the green are the hundreds of flowers, on hillsides and in meadows, singly and

NEW DIRECTIONS FOR PHILANTHROPIC FUNDRAISING, NO. 1, FALL 1993 © JOSSEY-BASS PUBLISHERS

in acrewide patches, and growing out of trees—from the tiny, almost shy, wild orchids, to the bold rhododendrons and azaleas, and the honeysuckle, which is smelled long before it is seen. If observers ever tired of looking at the trees and flowers, they could occupy themselves for hours with the birds and the animals. Most of us grew up hearing about the Appalachian mountains, and the many names given to different sections of the chain, from the Shenandoah to the Smokies, to the Cumberland.

But living in these mountains presents a less bucolic picture than reading about them or visiting the many tourist sites that make the Great Smoky Mountain National Park one of the most popular national parks in the United States. From the freeway, range after range of mountains are visible, along with odd squared-off hills devoid of vegetation, the remnants of the rampant strip mining that used to characterize this region. Getting off the freeway onto the less traveled side roads, one passes shack after shack, mobile homes turned into permanent housing, and an unusual number of landfills. Water that appears pristine from the road is visibly polluted up close. Household garbage is dumped by the side of the road or in the streams, and tires, old cars, sludge, and mounds of unidentifiable junk litter the roadsides. Some houses are built so close to the strip mines that the inhabitants walk out their doors and are in them.

In almost the entire Appalachian region, one out of seven homes has no running water, upward of 50 percent of the population is functionally illiterate, and unemployment varies from 10 to 50 percent. A high school diploma is thought of as highly as a college degree in more middle-class surroundings. Fewer people move in than leave, giving the region a population loss with each census. Those who leave often feel forced to move in order to get work or to build a better life for their children. Dubbed by many the "white Third World," Appalachia has the dubious distinction of being almost entirely white, with 80 percent of families living below the national poverty line. The area is largely rural; Knoxville, Tennessee (population 150,000) and Charleston, West Virginia (population 75,000) are among the biggest cities in the area. Many exciting organizations working for social justice have flourished here. Highlander Folk School (now called Highlander Research and Education Center) in New Market, Tennessee, celebrating its fifty-fifth anniversary, is probably the oldest. The Appalachian Peace Education Center in Abingdon, Virginia, and the Federation of Appalachian Housing Enterprises in Berea, Kentucky, are both just over ten years old.

History and operations of Save Our Cumberland Mountains

One of the oldest and most famous organizations in southern Appalachia is Save Our Cumberland Mountains (SOCM), located today in a small office in Lake City, Tennessee. SOCM was formed in 1972 to force local counties and the state of Tennessee to tax mine property and the value of minerals in land. At the time the group started, there were huge parcels of land, owned by coal companies, that were grossly undervalued by the property tax assessor due to the political influence of these companies. Income from property tax in many counties was negligible, leading to the poor quality of schools, or no schools at all in some counties. SOCM was successful in getting many counties to tax mine lands, and later it was able secure the passage of a "coal severance tax." SOCM began with a staff of two. Volunteers in Service to America (VISTA) contributed several staff to SOCM, until its virtual dismantling in 1981 by the Reagan administration.

Over the years, the SOCM staff has grown to eight, and its budget has expanded to $320,000. The extraordinary success of this organization, now celebrating its twentieth anniversary with a $500,000 "Year 2000" endowment campaign, has made SOCM a role model for many organizations in the region, and its story can only be helpful to others.

For the first ten years, SOCM existed by virtue of its popularity with foundations and the assistance of the VISTA staff. Membership dues provided minimal income, and other money was raised through special events. By keeping its budget low, SOCM stayed in the black, but there were still some very hard years. In 1981, the staff shrank from ten to five almost overnight with VISTA cuts; the loss of any foundation grants in various subsequent years could have sent the organization reeling.

Operated as a collective, each staff member earned $10,000 per year in 1985. Today, staff members earn $18,500 each. There is no extra pay for years of service. Until 1990, SOCM rented an office for $200 per month above a store in Jacksboro, Tennessee. Today, SOCM has an office in Lake City, costing around $600 per month, but cost control is still the hallmark of the organization.

SOCM's victories in the first ten years were impressive: regulating strip mining in the state of Tennessee, generating tax revenue, educating the public about strip and deep mining, and raising the issues of mining to a national level. Its work involved learning the very practical meanings of esoteric concepts such as surface rights and mineral rights, and broad-form deeds and reclamation. SOCM has always been a David to the Goliath of powerful mining companies and their interests, raising the specter of danger on occasion. In the early days, SOCM members had roofing nails thrown into their driveways, guaranteed to puncture tires or feet, and occasionally were shot at. Three members had their houses burned down. The violence was in part due to the rural nature of the work, which sometimes pitted family members against each other. For example, in one of the house burnings, the perpetrator was the cousin of the victim. Today, violence has given way to the more sophisticated strategies of job intimidation, fear of house repossession, denial of bank loans, and the like. These horrendous incidents attracted New York-based national foundations with an interest in Appalachia to SOCM. SOCM enjoys the support of many of its initial grantmakers to this day.

A series of coincidences helped SOCM avoid the pitfalls of relying entirely on foundation grants. The Youth Project (a national foundation more recently called Partnership for Democracy, which closed its doors in July 1992) had a field office in Knoxville. In 1980, the Youth Project recognized the danger that many of their grantees faced: overreliance on foundations for funding or, for some, the exact opposite, no foundation funding at all. The Youth Project contracted with Chicago-based fundraiser Joan Flanagan to research and write *The Grass Roots Fundraising Book*, which became an overnight classic (Flanagan, 1982). The book discusses how groups can become more financially self-sufficient through community-based fundraising strategies.

As a result of the book's popularity, Flanagan was much in demand as a trainer. She could not meet the demand for training, so the Youth Project received funding from the Mott Foundation and the National Institutes for Mental Health to conduct a "training-for-trainers" workshop. A dozen grass-roots fundraisers from around the country were brought to a retreat center in Minnesota for a week-long session, which was called the Self-Sufficiency Training Project. The trainers included Flanagan, Si Kahn (a longtime organizer from North Carolina), Karen Thompson (Midwest Academy), and Hulbert James (then at the Youth Project). The main brain behind the idea was Mary Harrington, who was head of the project. Included among the trainees were David Dotson from the Knoxville Youth Project; Peggy Mathews, an organizer and fundraiser from SOCM; and myself, then a fundraiser for the Coalition for the Medical Rights of Women (CMRW) in San Francisco. There were many other organizers there, but the three of us became friends almost instantly. The training explored a range of strategies, many of which were impractical for SOCM to implement. Door-to-door canvassing, an excellent strategy for cities and towns, was out of the question because of the distance between doors in rural areas. Large-scale direct mail was inappropriate because of the lack of population. Even the staging of more than a few special events was difficult because of the distances that people had to travel. The emphasis at the training was very much on special events. CMRW had placed its emphasis on major donors, which was a new strategy for almost everyone else there. Major-donor solicitation required only a few people, which made it a great rural strategy. The tasks of finding prospects, cultivating their interests, and asking for large gifts posed challenges, but not insurmountable obstacles. SOCM was very attracted to the notion of building an individual donor base, and to utilizing membership dues and contributions as a fundraising strategy as much as an organizing strategy. Since the Youth Project was a major advocate for SOCM, I was able to start helping them.

In 1983, I made my first trip to SOCM. I had become a full-time fundraising trainer as a result of the training-for-trainers workshop and had lined up several client groups, who were together splitting my costs. I spent half a day with SOCM in their dusty, paper-filled office. Financial self-sufficiency by raising money from individuals was very appealing to their fundraiser, Peggy Mathews, and to other staff as well. Although they were skeptical of the strategy's transferability from San Francisco, they were willing to give this type of fundraising a try. SOCM became the first rural group among my clients to implement the individual donor strategies that I taught them.

Their first effort in working on major donors entailed an exciting and bold challenge from one of their original staff, Boomer Winfrey. Winfrey is a Renaissance man. He is a newspaper publisher, organizer, and canoe expert. He proposed and carried out a "canoe-a-thon," canoeing from Norris Dam (outside Lake City) to the Everglades, a distance of eighteen hundred miles. People pledged a certain amount per mile. He sent monthly letters to his sponsors, who kept the excitement going for the whole trip. The canoe-a-thon netted $12,000, with a couple of people pledging as much as a dollar per mile! This was a great achievement for this small group, demonstrating that they were capable of attracting fairly large gifts.

In 1987, to celebrate their fifteenth anniversary, SOCM again created an unusual fundraising event. The organization had accomplished a fair degree of fiscal stability. As a result, its work was rarely stopped by cash flow problems or financial crises. However, it sometimes was hampered by the lack of a large amount of money to do something bold. For example, in some of its work, SOCM goes to the courts to seek justice. They must rely on pro bono lawyers, and they have several excellent volunteer attorneys. However, sometimes pro bono lawyers cannot put the necessary time into a case or the case drags on past what is possible to expect from lawyers who are working for free. With an infusion of money, SOCM could occasionally hire a lawyer. Also, campaigns were sometimes stymied due to insufficient funds to rent buses and take dozens of people to Nashville for lobbying, or to go all-out with a letter-writing or telephone campaign. To respond to this need, SOCM created the Can Do It Fund so that they would not be hindered in their work by a lack of funds. Funds would be available for lobbying or direct action or whatever—no strings attached. The fundraising campaign goal was set for $45,000, which was $3,000 for every year of SOCM's existence. Quilts, which were produced by a local self-help project, were given to all donors who made gifts of $1,500 and up. Artist Gabriel Marie Hoare created a print featuring a lyric from the Si Kahn song "People Like You Help People Like Me Go On, Go On" for those who gave $75 and up, and a quilted square wall hanging was given to donors of $400 ($100 per quarter). SOCM reached its goal! By now the board was much more involved in fundraising, and all of the staff members were asking individuals for large gifts. Most of the $45,000 came from gifts of $50 or more. Although many people received personal visits, the bulk of the fundraising was conducted through small-scale direct mail and personal letters.

SOCM realized that it could not solely depend on people in the local community for support. There simply were not enough people, and very few locals had the money to make large gifts. They began soliciting nationally for support. One very creative annual fundraising effort was started by Heleny Cook in Washington, D.C. She had worked with SOCM as its first staff organizer. Cook rents a small boat club on the Potomac and invites all of her friends, former SOCM volunteers, and the general public for an annual crabfest. Boiled crabs and beer form the base of the menu, and an auction of items such as moonshine and Appalachian crafts has become a tradition. Most of the costs are underwritten by a few people, who are contacted each year to foot the bills for this event. People have a really good time at the event, and $5,000 is netted each year for SOCM.

First steps in building a major-donor base

One of the first steps in building a donor base is to define a major donor. For SOCM, as with many grass-roots groups, a major donor is classified as anyone giving $50 or more. Even with a major-donor category set that low, the pool of prospects is limited considerably. SOCM operates in a region where $25 is a lot of money for most residents. However, prospect lists were developed, and staff and a few board members started soliciting donations. In the first two years, asking was almost entirely done by mail, with some telephone follow-ups. Distance was often named as the reason for this approach. However, since organizers traveled hundreds of miles weekly to talk with people in their homes to build a better organization, the distance question was clearly an excuse. As with staffs and board members of every group that I have ever known, the people at SOCM felt very uncomfortable about asking for money. The Appalachian mountain culture places more emphasis on politeness than does the rest of the country, and the SOCM people feared that those from whom they solicited donations would be unable to say no. Askers were worried that they might be imposing on people or embarrassing them—standard fundraising fears!

There was an added and very unspoken fear of finding someone who could donate a significant sum. Somehow, taking large amounts of money from foundations did not raise this fear of control. What if someone in the community gave $5,000 or $2,500? What would he or she want in return? What kind of accountability does an organization have to major donors? To be fair, the SOCM staff members were always overworked, and weighing a drive of two hours to ask for $100 against two hours of work on a grant proposal that could yield $15,000 was an easy choice to make. Also, proposals come with deadlines, but donors rarely impose deadlines ("You must come and ask me by May 1 or else"). Since the staff had had great success in obtaining foundation grants, there was less incentive initially to devote precious time to major-donor fundraising, which was still untested. The fundraising staff person was able to spend only 20 percent of her time on major donors, and the rest of the staff much less. With two or three board members involved, however, SOCM was still consistently able to raise $25,000 to $30,000 every year, starting in 1985.

My experience as a donor to SOCM provides insight into how the organization initially worked with its donors. When I first consulted with SOCM, I gave them $25 for a membership. I liked them a lot, and I mentioned them to other groups. The next time I consulted with them, I stayed with their fundraiser, Alison Taylor. During the course of my day with the staff, I had talked about the importance of the staff and board making their own gifts, and that to be a good fundraiser, one had to be a good giver. We discussed how much a person should give, and I mentioned that I gave 10 percent of my income. Several hours later, we were reviewing how to identify a prospect and how to decide how much to ask. I talked about the gift range chart and about looking at a person's income and lifestyle. People still felt uncertain about how to determine how much a person might earn, so I led them through an exercise to figure out how much someone earned in a year, using myself as the guinea pig. Through this exercise, they determined my income.

That evening, sitting with Taylor, sipping some Tennessee bourbon, she asked me to give $500 to SOCM. I had never given that large a gift, and so I asked her how she arrived at the amount. She said she had done what I told her: Pay attention to what people say about themselves. She said, "You said SOCM is one of your favorite groups, so your gift to SOCM should be one of your biggest gifts. You said you give away 10 percent of your gross income, and we figured out your income." That year I had earned $30,000 and given away $3,000, and Taylor reckoned $500 should accurately reflect how much I cared about SOCM. I had to agree. Surprising myself,

I gave the money. I moved to Tennessee shortly after that, and the next year gave the same amount.

In 1987, I consulted with them about their fifteenth anniversary. I suggested (without realizing what this would mean to me) that they go to their biggest donors and ask them to give some amount for each year of SOCM's existence. For example, a staff member could ask someone for $100 per year or $50 per year, but it had to be more (preferably, much more) than the individual was giving already. By now, Vicki Quatmann was the fundraiser, and she took this message to heart and asked me for $100 for each year SOCM had existed. The sum of $1,500 broke another barrier in my giving. But I gave it. I was making more money, and it followed that I should give more. I also threw a party for SOCM in conjunction with my birthday and asked people to give SOCM donations instead of birthday gifts to me. The party netted $1,500. The following year, I intended to go back to giving $500, but, at some point, Quatmann and another staff member attended a training session that I conducted for the general nonprofit community. During that training, I said that when a person makes a really substantial gift as a special donation in one year, and he or she is able to pay it all during that year, a group should consider asking that person for the same gift again. "Perhaps what the donor learned is that he or she could afford to make such a big gift every year," I said. A few months after this training, Quatmann asked me to renew my annual gift to SOCM and to consider giving $1,500. "Perhaps," she said, "you have discovered that you can make this kind of gift every year." I was actually flabbergasted but realized that I could afford it. I had not gone without anything I needed to give that much. I gave it again.

In 1989, I moved to New York City, and, early in 1990, SOCM implemented another fundraising principle: Get the board members to ask. Michael Hodge, a long-time activist and then chair of the SOCM board, sent me a four-page handwritten letter about SOCM's accomplishments and asking me to renew at $1,500. The letter was magnificent, and a few days later, as promised, Hodge called. He said that making the call was very hard because I had been his fundraising teacher. I found his technique flawless—honest, straightforward, friendly, down to earth, and disingenuous. I gave $1,500 again.

I gave that amount every year until 1992, when SOCM launched its Year 2000 Fund and I pledged $5,000, which will be paid over a couple of years. This request was made by my longtime friend, and still SOCM's fundraiser, Vicki Quatmann. As of May 1993, 150 donors have pledged $150,000 to SOCM's Year 2000 Fund, nearly all of them individuals with very modest incomes. The goal is to raise $500,000 over a three-year period. Interest income from the fund will be used to support SOCM's efforts to recruit a more diverse membership and to become a citizen's organization for all rural Tennesseans. Before the campaign is over, each of the 1,300 member families will be asked to make a three-year pledge. Nearly all of the 150 pledgers are sending their gifts to SOCM in monthly or quarterly installments. The monthly reminder system has made it possible for many to give gifts much larger than they ever before thought possible.

Ten important lessons

My years with SOCM have taught me ten important lessons about fundraising that apply to most groups. I list them in the order that I learned them and the order in which I believe SOCM learned them. Whether one or another point is more or less important depends on the organization. I think that all of these principles are equally important and that they provide a useful frame of reference against which to measure fundraising progress.

First, to be successful, an organization's leadership has to understand that a diverse funding base is integral to an organization's independence and stability, and that people will feel a greater ownership of an organization when they become both givers and askers themselves. Unfortunately, many do not take these necessary steps until there is a crisis. SOCM understands this philosophy: In order for

the organization to be truly run by members, and to truly empower people who have been systematically disenfranchised for generations, it must belong to its members. They should be able to hire
and fire staff, set policy or choose organizing efforts, select new
board members from among themselves, and speak to legislators or
reporters themselves rather than have staff do it. All of these points
are important, but without control of money, without enough money
coming from members and raised by members, members still lack
power. When members understand this fact, they are motivated to
fundraise in the same way that they are moved to work on issues.
Often, in Appalachia, people must overcome profound cultural and
class taboos to raise funds.

Second, the leadership of an organization does not need to wait
to act until everyone agrees with or understands the need for financial diversity or has the understanding mentioned above. In fact, if
the group waits that long, it could fold. This is an evolutionary
process. As many people as want to can engage in fundraising. In
SOCM's case, a handful of staff pursued individual donors, followed
(with some reluctance) by the rest of the staff, picking up a few board
members here and there, and, almost ten years later, followed by
the majority of the board.

Third, an infrastructure must be in place in order to build an individual donor base. Record keeping must be excellent, and systems
must be in place to thank people, place them on the mailing list, and
track their gifts. Computers have made these tasks much simpler,
but computers cannot replace human ingenuity and perseverance,
attention to detail, and willingness to do the seemingly unexciting
and unglamorous work of record keeping.

Fourth, the organization must be trained by a trusted outside consultant. This training has to extend over a period of years. The group
is first trained in fundraising principles then given a few months or
even years to implement the training. The consultant returns for
follow-up and fine-tuning, as well as to offer inspiration and praise
for what has been achieved so far. SOCM was fortunate to have sev-

eral consultants over the years, including myself, and established warm relationships with them.

Fifth, the group must evaluate its progress realistically and set goals that make sense. A major failing of many groups is that they set their goals too high and then beat themselves up for not making the goals. A goal should involve some tolerance of risk in order to be worth striving for, but it should not be foolish. Many factors have to be taken into account in setting goals, such as past fundraising history and the number of people able and willing to work on fundraising. SOCM generally sets low-to-moderate goals, drawing on their experience as organizers to pick issues that they can win on, or to break issues down into winnable parts. In their most recent and most ambitious effort to raise $500,000, they hired a consulting firm to conduct a feasibility study. The firm interviewed all SOCM donors who had given $250 or more per year and new prospects as well to determine a feasible monetary goal for the campaign.

Sixth, fundraising must be spread over a number of people. In *Profiles of Excellence: Achieving Success in the Nonprofit Sector*, Knauft, Berger, and Gray (1991) researched groups over five years and concluded that there were four hallmarks of excellence in nonprofit organizations: (1) a clearly articulated sense of mission that serves as the focal point of commitment for board and staff, (2) an individual who truly leads the organization and creates a culture that enables and motivates the organization to fulfill its mission, (3) an involved and committed volunteer board, and (4) an ongoing capacity to attract sufficient financial and human resources.

For three of these characteristics, I wholeheartedly agree, but I totally disagree with the inclusion of the second feature. Organizations in which one individual plays this vital role are accidents waiting to happen. While there are important and inspiring people among us, the hallmark of a successful organization is that its most important people are primarily engaged in the process of distributing power among many people, and each individual is engaged, in part, in the process of making himself or herself dispensable. Certainly, this is the case at SOCM, where there are moderate staff turnover and new board members every two years. There is an infusion of new people as new SOCM chapters are organized and as new issues are taken on.

Seventh, there has to be a willingness to suspend disbelief. SOCM was initially skeptical of the newly suggested fundraising strategies. They had not previously been tried in the SOCM setting, and there were many reasons to think that they would fail. Nevertheless, SOCM gave it a shot.

Eighth, there has to be a capacity for delayed gratification. It has been ten years since our original training. SOCM is only now able to undertake a $500,000 campaign. This has been a slow and evolutionary process. As Buddhist philosophy expresses, "We have so little time, we must proceed very slowly."

Ninth, the people in the group must like and respect each other and have a mutual sense of fun. While they do not all need to be best friends or socialize together, there must be times for socializing and shared group experiences that are not work related. These periods will allow people to overlook or forgive tension in their work and trust each other for feedback, even during disagreements. SOCM staff go on one rafting trip each year together. The trip takes three or four days and provides a way for staff members to get to know one another outside of work.

Tenth, there have to be enough fundraisers, and board members should be first on the list. As Vicki Quatmann says, "Save time and ask the people closest to the group first. Ask them right. Go to their homes and sit in their living rooms and talk about the work and the campaign. People will dig deep. They like that attention, and it brings them right into the group." She feels that if SOCM could start all over again, this tenth principle would be first. When we first thought of doing major-donor fundraising at SOCM, we imagined that we would not have enough prospects. In fact, the problem has been too few askers. By bringing the board in early, using the technique of personal solicitation on them first, we could have had more askers working sooner.

Conclusion

Of course, a major cornerstone of all effective fundraising is that the group must be worth raising money for and that staff, board members, volunteers, and members must all know, believe in, and own the mission of the organization. SOCM's mission keeps people's eyes on the prize, so it is fitting to end this chapter with that organization's mission statement:

We Believe

We believe that each of us has an inherent power and right to affect the course of our lives and surroundings. We are committed to using this power to improve the quality of life in our communities.

We believe that we have a right to know about and have a voice in developments which will affect the quality of life in our communities.

We believe that those who come into our communities to engage in enterprises have a responsibility to be sensitive to the wishes of those who live in the community and to carry their fair share of civic responsibilities.

We believe that there is strength in organization, in people working together to protect their rights and seek improvements in their communities.

References

Flanagan, J. *The Grass Roots Fundraising Book: How to Raise Money in Your Community*. Chicago: Contemporary Books, 1982.

Knauft, E. B., Berger, R. A., and Gray, S. T. *Profiles of Excellence: Achieving Success in the Nonprofit Sector*. San Francisco: Jossey-Bass, 1991.

KIM KLEIN, *consultant and trainer, is author of* Fundraising for Social Change *(Inverness, Calif.: Chardon Press) and publisher of the* Grassroots Fundraising Journal *(Berkeley, Calif.).*

*After the Watts riots in 1965, a group of black com-
munity activists created the Brotherhood Crusade
to raise funds to support their community's institutions and to empower other blacks to improve their
socioeconomic status. Their efforts inspired a national movement, the National Black United Fund,
which raised over $7 million in 1990 and opened
up America's workplaces for fundraising by black
organizations and other groups.*

4

The National Black United Fund:
From movement for social change
to social change organization

Emmett D. Carson

*This chapter represents the views of the author and not those of the Ford
Foundation. The author thanks the National Black United Fund for making all of its files available as well as the numerous individuals who con-
sented to be interviewed.*

THERE ARE OVER 983,000 nonprofit tax-exempt organizations in the
United States (Hodgkinson, Weitzman, Toppe, and Noga, 1992,
p. 4). While nearly all of these organizations have made a difference
in the lives of individuals, few have influenced the development of
the nonprofit sector as a whole. There are even fewer organizations
that have embodied a community's aspirations for self-determina-

tion, and fewer still that can claim a large share of the credit in demonstrating how other segments of society might duplicate their organizational models to achieve their own aspirations. It is these accomplishments that make the National Black United Fund (NBUF) an important and unique institution for a case study analysis.

NBUF, located in Newark, New Jersey, was founded in 1972. Today, it is a federation consisting of fifteen independent fundraising organizations located throughout the United States, each of which raises and distributes monies to charitable organizations. In 1990, NBUF and its affiliates raised over $7 million, 50 percent of which was distributed as direct grants to nonprofit organizations, 30 percent to program projects, and 20 percent to fundraising and administrative costs. The majority of these funds were raised through participation in work-site charitable payroll deduction plans. However, from 1974, when NBUF was formally announced, to 1982, when its primary founder died, NBUF was more than just a black charitable federation; it was a vibrant movement for social change.

This chapter examines how NBUF's mission and its decision to pursue access to the work-site charitable payroll deduction plans of the federal government and private employers influenced its subsequent organizational development from a movement for social change to a social change organization. My research draws on several sources of information, including NBUF's internal files, published magazine and newspaper articles, and interviews with several key individuals who are familiar with NBUF's early development. By examining NBUF's mission and the activities that it developed in support of its mission, my aim is to characterize how other organizations can continue to duplicate its many successes and avoid its pitfalls.

At the outset, it is important to note that this chapter is not intended as a comprehensive analysis of either NBUF's development or its leaders. While such an undertaking is certainly warranted given NBUF's historical significance and continuing importance, the effort falls outside of the more narrow scope of this study.

NBUF's origins

To accurately understand the dynamics that led to the creation of NBUF, it is essential to discuss the Brotherhood Crusade, located in Los Angeles, California, which was started in 1968 (Davis, 1982). In many ways, the Brotherhood Crusade was a miniature working model for what would become NBUF. Following the Watts riots of 1965, a group of black community activists, led by Walter Bremond, determined that if blacks were to empower themselves to improve their socioeconomic status, they would need to develop a systematic process or mechanism through which to financially support their own institutions.

The idea of black Americans engaging in charitable activities to help themselves is certainly not new. The history of black self-help dates back over two hundred years to the first black churches and mutual aid societies (Carson, 1989, 1991, 1993). These organizations provided important services that blacks were denied from receiving from government agencies and most, although not all, charitable organizations that served the white community. Moreover, black philanthropy provided the financial and volunteer resources needed to sustain such national social protest movements as the Underground Railroad, the Marcus Garvey movement, and the civil rights movement. What distinguished the Brotherhood Crusade was its effort to develop a systematic method of raising money, similar in some respects to tithing through the church, from people who did not know each other but who shared a common value of wanting to provide assistance to their community.

The Brotherhood Crusade was successful in several respects. The effort proved, despite a number of failed attempts between 1954 and 1966, that a diverse cross section of the black community would support an independent black charitable organization advocating a social change agenda. Further, the Brotherhood Crusade determined that a crucial element of its mission was to educate the black community about the importance of financial control of their own institutions. Finally, as discussed later, the Brotherhood Crusade settled on work-site charitable payroll deduction plans as the preferred method of fundraising.

The philosophy of blacks helping other blacks became the hallmark of NBUF's approach to philanthropy as exemplified by its motto, The Helping Hand That Is Your Own. This appeal for race-based support created continuous questions and concerns both within and outside the black community about whether NBUF's self-help activities represented black self-determination, which should be encouraged, or black separatism, which should be opposed.

It should be noted that not all of the local black federated campaigns agreed with NBUF's black self-help philosophy. Perhaps the most well-known person who disagreed was Calvin W. Rolark, who founded the United Black Fund (UBF) of Washington, D.C., in 1969 and the United Black Fund of America in 1977. While personal recollections differ, it has been said that Rolark declined to join NBUF, in part because of his belief that black organizations should be open to accepting money from multiple sources, including United Way.

UBF's partnership with United Way ("United Black Fund," 1984, p. 12) was an arrangement that NBUF was offered several times and steadfastly refused on philosophical grounds as antithetical to NBUF's mission of promoting black self-help. The central issue for NBUF was not the race of the contributor per se but rather who would have control over the organization's financial health and stability and whether that constituency supported NBUF's self-help philosophy. NBUF believed that money from mainstream institutions, such as United Way, that dictated program directions and activities would never allow NBUF to challenge the basic power relationships that the organization felt limited black socioeconomic advancement and that it was committed to changing.

Notwithstanding statements from NBUF's leadership that support of black self-determination in the form of black financial and volunteer support did not preclude support from nonblack individuals or institutions, NBUF had to constantly rebut charges of promoting black separatism (Joseph, 1976, p. 8). Over time however, the clear line that NBUF's leaders articulated between black self-determination and black separatism eventually became more difficult to discern, especially in the heated exchanges that ensued over NBUF's efforts to gain access to various workplace charitable deduction campaigns.

Lifeline from the Cummins Engine Foundation

During NBUF's early years, the Cummins Engine Foundation, under the leadership of James A. Joseph, played a critical role. Like all new organizations, NBUF faced the problem of raising start-up funds to begin its operations. What made this especially difficult was the dilemma of how to raise such funds given NBUF's black self-help philosophy. After all, it was not likely that many foundations and corporations would support an organization committed to altering the traditional power relationships, and the local Black United Funds (BUFs) that were then emerging did not generate sufficient resources to support themselves and a national office.

In 1972, James Joseph joined the Cummins Engine Foundation as its president. One of his key program initiatives was to influence philanthropy from a black perspective. As part of this effort, the Cummins Engine Foundation hired six locally based program officers to stimulate black self-help and empowerment activities in Atlanta, Baltimore, Chicago, Detroit, Los Angeles, and Washington, D.C. Walter Bremond was hired as the program officer for Los Angeles. As part of his responsibilities, Bremond was to develop and organize NBUF. Later, as NBUF's executive director, Bremond continued to receive his salary from the Cummins Engine Foundation to run NBUF. This arrangement was not unusual for the Cummins Engine Foundation at that time, since it also supported similar arrangements with the Association of Black Foundation Executives and the Black Women's Community Development Foundation.

The close relationship between NBUF and the Cummins Engine

Foundation was no doubt facilitated by the fact that James Joseph served as the president of NBUF's first board of directors. The financial and in-kind support that the Cummins Engine Foundation provided NBUF during its early development was critical in that it allowed NBUF to become operational. This support also enabled the organization, at least temporarily, to put aside the philosophical dilemma of how to start and maintain a social movement dedicated to black self-help without becoming compromised by financial assistance from the very institutions and structures that the organization sought to change. While NBUF did receive support from other foundations (for example, the Lilly Endowment and the Ford Foundation), such support did not match the substantial long-term commitment of the Cummins Engine Foundation.

NBUF's dual mission: A delicate balancing act

There is a growing acceptance in the literature on nonprofit organizational management that a nonprofit organization's mission is a key factor in understanding its accomplishments or shortcomings (Drucker, 1990, pp. 7–8; Bryce, 1992, pp. 66–67). From its inception, NBUF saw itself as having two distinct missions. Bremond stated that the organization's mission was to promote the development of local affiliate BUFs and, even more important, to refine and promote the concept and method of black self-help. To achieve this dual mission, Bremond (1976, p. 12) described ten goals for NBUF, four of which are critical to understanding its later organizational development: "to assist local groups in the creation and establishment of local Black United Funds"; "to provide technical assistance to local Black United Funds"; "to interpret clearly that Black United Funds are not established as a negative or confrontation vehicle against United Funds [United Way] on local or national levels, but as a positive response to financial and program needs of the black community"; and "to establish a dialogue with other national organizations to evaluate the trends that have had an impact on the lives of black people."

NBUF encountered at least two areas of tension in pursuing these goals. (The word *tension* is used here to suggest that a delicate balance must be maintained between different constituencies with different expectations.) First, as discussed earlier, NBUF had to clearly delineate and explain its philosophy of black self-determination and empowerment, as distinguished from black separatism. Second, there was an inherent tension between NBUF's desire to start and assist local BUFs and its desire to create a national dialogue on the socioeconomic status of black Americans.

The issue here is not that these goals were overly ambitious for a newly formed organization but rather that achievement of both goals, including support of the activities related to each over time, would be extremely difficult. More specifically, NBUF would have to involve two very different constituencies—those concerned with advancing the social movement and those interested in developing local BUFs—who would ultimately view NBUF in fundamentally different ways. The tensions inherent to NBUF's multiple objectives did not necessarily mean that NBUF had embarked on an impossible assignment. On the contrary, what is remarkable is that for nearly ten years NBUF was able to make significant progress in both areas.

From movement for social change to social change organization

From its very beginning, what set NBUF apart was its philosophy that black Americans needed to provide financial and volunteer support for their own institutions in order to address the fundamental causes of social inequity within U.S. society. James Joseph described NBUF's role in the following way: "The Black community needs social action, and when you support social action, you are supporting potentially controversial, high-risk charitable activity. The traditional charitable agencies have not been interested in supporting potentially controversial social action. The Black community knows it must deal with the basic problem facing the Black community—and that can be defined as the inequitable distribution of power and resources in society. So what we [NBUF] seek is a fundamental rearrangement of power relationships. We know that it is going to be difficult to find outside resources to direct at that basic problem" (Jenkins, 1977, p. 49).

NBUF's perception of itself as a new black movement for social change was confirmed by the prominent and diverse group of blacks who agreed to serve on its eighty-eight member national governing board and to participate in its national conferences some years later. During its early years, NBUF's board roster read like a *Who's Who of Black America:* the Reverend Negail Riley, Dorothy Height, Reverend Leon Sullivan, Hank Aaron, Quincy Jones, Bishop John Hurst Adams, Imamu Amiri Baraka, Tony Brown, Benjamin Hooks, Congressman Charles Rangel, the Reverend Jesse Jackson, and Lerone Bennett, among others. From all accounts, it was Bremond's charismatic and visionary leadership that was able to attract and unify these prominent, strong-willed board members, representing diverse interests in the black community, to NBUF's cause. It is important to note that NBUF's board not only represented the black middle class but also made considerable efforts to involve all socioeconomic segments of the black community.

The primary way in which NBUF attempted to create a national dialogue on issues of concern to the black community was through its annual public policy conferences. These conferences drew large audiences to hear nationally known speakers and generated widespread press coverage. The success of these conferences reinforced NBUF's desire to raise larger social issues related to black America rather than to be simply another charitable fundraising organization. Describing the mood of one conference, a reporter wrote, "The conference was like a rebirth. Many of the old soldiers of the '60s—older, fatter, better fed—emerged from all corners of the nation to express themselves. There was a spirit and a vitality; and electricity in the air that reflected a new call to battle. There was a briskness in people's walks, a determination in people's eyes, and a firmness on people's faces that reflected the seriousness of the four-day involvement" (Griffin, 1978, p. 49).

Despite the success of these conferences, they were costly and did not generate enough revenue to be self-financing. In addition, the conferences required substantial staff time for planning, organization, and fundraising. Some board members believed that the time and money could be better used to strengthen local BUFs. However, Bremond's vision and ability to raise funds for the conferences allowed him to prevail in this matter.

Collapse of the movement

The movement nature of NBUF presented a number of unique challenges to NBUF's organizational structure. Recall that NBUF was formed from several preexisting organizations. Over time, these local BUFs, as well as the new BUFs that NBUF helped to create, began to have organizational and technical assistance needs and concerns that were separate and distinct from concerns related to the proliferation of NBUF as a movement for social change. However, the principal interest of the majority of NBUF's board members was not to serve the technical assistance needs of local BUFs but rather to assist NBUF in creating a national debate on public policy issues of importance to black America. In its initial years of operation, NBUF received a disproportionate share of its revenue from a small number of foundations and corporations (Jenkins, 1977, p. 24). As noted earlier, a substantial portion of this support was from the Cummins Engine Foundation. In the late 1970s, however, foundation and corporate support for NBUF began to decline. This was due to a combination of factors.

First, it is likely that a number of foundations and corporations felt uncomfortable with NBUF's decision to bring a legal suit to gain access to federal workplace charitable payroll deduction campaigns and to lobby through black employees to gain access to private workplace campaigns. Many of these institutions had had a long relationship with United Way, and charges by NBUF that United Way did not equitably serve all segments of society, particularly the black community, were sure to alienate some quarters of the business and philanthropic community that supported United Way through grants or held their own United Way workplace campaigns. Second, there is evidence that NBUF's administrative record keeping at the time was occasionally lax in terms of compliance with foundation reporting requirements, which would have made applications for subsequent grants more difficult. Finally, many foundations have policies that limit the length of time over which a project can be supported. So, after several years of support, the handful of foundations that had been NBUF donors began to reduce or end their support as a matter of policy. With regard to the Cummins Engine Foundation, James Joseph resigned as president in 1979 to become undersecretary of the Department of the Interior, thereby effectively severing that institution's close relationship with NBUF.

A greater proportion of NBUF's revenue began to come from local BUFs as foundation support declined, and the board members representing local BUFs were able to exert more influence over NBUF's activities and direction. It was not that the local BUF board members did not support the notion of a NBUF movement for social change; they did. But when faced with the expense of supporting their own fledgling independent local organizations and the choice of whether to provide NBUF with limited resources either to strengthen the capacities of local BUFs or to underwrite national conferences and related activities that promulgated the movement, they were more willing to support the technical assistance activities.

NBUF's shift from a movement for social change to a social change organization was solidified in 1982 with Bremond's unexpected death at age forty-eight from a heart attack (Bothwell and Saasta, 1982). His death created a leadership vacuum that led to a protracted internal battle for control of the organization by board members representing different factions of the local BUFs. Bremond's death also marked the gradual departure of nearly all of the more prominent board members who had been drawn to NBUF because of his vision of a new black movement for social change and their personal relationships with him.

Payroll deduction: The preferred fundraising method

While there was disagreement within NBUF about the relative value of the public policy conferences, there was widespread consensus, though for different reasons, for the decision to pursue strategies to gain access to work-site charitable payroll deduction plans. It is important to realize that, at its founding, NBUF had not yet determined the primary mechanism through which it would solicit monies from black donors to distribute to black organizations. At least part of NBUF's search for an efficient mechanism to solicit money was aided by the Brotherhood Crusade when it successfully petitioned and became a participating member of Los Angeles's charitable work-site payroll deduction campaign. Daniel Bakewell (1976, p. 23), one of the Brotherhood Crusade's founders, recalled the impact that this achievement had on both the Brotherhood Crusade and NBUF: "In its fourth year of operation, the Brotherhood Crusade organizers decided that to be a viable force within the community required pursuing an independent and perpetual source of support—not tied to foundations or grants. Such a realization forced the Crusade to develop and implement a payroll deduction program. . . . The development of a city-backed payroll deduction program was the principal action that established the prevailing fundraising strategy not only for the Crusade, but for all other local black fundraising organizations across the country."

NBUF's decision to replicate the Crusade's fundraising strategy at the national level by pursuing access to the Combined Federal Campaign (CFC) brought it into direct conflict with United Way and its supporters. The decision to challenge the policies governing access to CFC brought both constituencies of NBUF's dual mission into agreement. For those concerned with NBUF as a movement, the challenge represented a monumental contest reminiscent of

David versus Goliath that was consistent with NBUF's mission to alter existing power relationships. For those concerned with NBUF as a viable black charitable federation, access to CFC would ensure a steady stream of revenue and would create opportunities to develop local BUFs in cities across the United States where there were large black populations.

Struggle for equal access

The fundamental argument for United Way's monopoly access to the workplace, now as always, is based on efficiency. A single organization, proponents argue, more efficiently handles administrative and operations costs and is therefore free to apply a greater percentage of the money raised to providing services than can be achieved by smaller organizations. Further, the simultaneous raising and administering of funds by many smaller organizations would entail costly duplication of effort.

What is seldom acknowledged about the efficiency argument and what NBUF and others raised in their efforts to gain access to CFC and other workplace campaigns is that the efficiency argument is valid only to the extent that the large charitable federation provides the *same* set of services as the smaller charitable federations would provide. In fact, two problems have emerged over time that concern the structure of United Way.

First, as Bremond frequently noted, the local service agencies that were the earliest United Way members (and therefore the earliest to qualify for allocations) in a given community have continued to receive the lion's share of the fundraising pot, leaving little behind for the newer organizations that are more likely to represent minorities' and women's interests or the concerns of special interest groups. This skewed distribution of funds tends to discourage additional charitable organizations from joining (Palmer, 1977). Further, the fact that newer charitable organizations are more apt to represent nontraditional interests has been another source of conflict in allocation choices (National Committee for Responsive Philanthropy, 1986, pp. 28–34).

Another kind of efficiency often mentioned in defense of single-organization access concerns the ability to raise the greatest sum possible at the workplace. This argument rests on the inaccurate belief that the innate level of generosity is limited, so that if more fundraising organizations are allowed to participate in a company's campaign, less money will be donated to the organizations that had preceded them as participants. In fact, research indicates that the practice of allowing more organizations access to private payroll deduction plans actually increases the number of employees who participate, raising the total amount of money contributed (Polivy, 1985). Moreover, it appears that not only do blacks and whites have different giving priorities, but blacks are more likely than whites to participate in work-site charitable payroll deduction plans (Carson, 1988; Witty, 1989).

Given this background, NBUF's decision to legally challenge United Way's sole access to CFC in 1976 was nothing less than monumental. What is not generally known is that the Cummins Engine Foundation paid the retainer of the law firm that prepared and filed NBUF's legal suit against CFC. For its members, NBUF's decision reinforced the perception of NBUF as a movement dedicated to challenging fundamental power relationships. For others, NBUF's efforts to become part of CFC were perceived as an attempt to undermine and discredit United Way and, by implication, its supporters by challenging the veracity of United Way's assertions that all groups benefited equally from its efforts. As a result, NBUF was challenged by both mainstream and black institutions.

The lack of support for NBUF, and, in some quarters, opposition from several national black civil rights and social change organizations, reflected a number of issues. First, several of these organizations received support from United Way, corporate friends of United Way, or both and felt compelled to support United Way's position so that they would not jeopardize their own financial support. Second, some of these institutions felt that NBUF was directly challenging their leadership position within the black community by holding its annual public policy conferences and creating a national debate about black self-help and empowerment. Third, and the most troubling suggestion, some of the leaders of these organizations may have doubted the capacity and accountability of blacks to successfully develop and manage so complex an endeavor (Davis, 1975, pp. 143–144).

To NBUF's credit, the organization's leadership tried to resist attempts to depict its efforts to gain access to CFC as an attack on United Way's operations. NBUF began its effort by stressing that its concern was a policy issue related to United Way's sole access to CFC and not a matter of how United Way distributed the money. However, as tensions over this issue escalated, and United Way and its supporters continued to resist NBUF's efforts to gain access to CFC, Bremond did begin to make public statements about the efficacy of United Way's programs in relation to black Americans.

Speaking at a conference in 1978 on fundraising in the workplace, Bremond delivered a blistering speech to the conferees on the United Way monopoly. In his opening remarks, he directly challenged United Way's assertion of supporting all groups equally: "But behind United Way's sentimental slogan appeal to 'Give Once for All,' are cold, contradictory realities which evidence exclusionary admission practices, exclusionary giving patterns, and antiquated priorities. We have heard a lot about United Way's infatuation with funding only noncontroversial organizations. . . . And there are many other examples of United Way's arrogant practices against agencies struggling to provide services to needy people. And certainly, the relationship that United Way has had with Black America is one characterized by paternalism, institutional racism, and a peculiar form of arrogance indicative of an era when this country was run by plantation owners" (Bremond, 1978, p. 1).

The sentiments expressed in Bremond's speech indicate the "them or us" proposition that NBUF would begin to use to distinguish supporters from detractors in its confrontation with United Way. At best, this position began to blur the careful distinctions that

NBUF had earlier articulated between black self-determination and black separatism. At worst, for some, it crossed the line in a manner that would make NBUF even more difficult to politically, financially, or philosophically support.

NBUF's legal victory in obtaining access to CFC (*NBUF v. Campbell*, 494 F. Supp. 748, 1980), as well as the NAACP Legal Defense Fund's successful suit (*NAACP Legal Defense Fund v. Campbell*, 504 F. Supp. 1365, 1981), served to open the charitable marketplace to a wide variety of special purpose organizations (National Committee for Responsive Philanthropy, 1986, pp. 24–57). These organizations included women's funds, Latino funds, and environmental funds, among others (National Committee for Responsive Philanthropy, 1986, pp. 42–62). However, despite its legal victory in 1980, NBUF did not gain access to CFC until two years later, after a number of other groups were admitted into the campaign, due to regulations developed by the federal government that prohibited participation in CFC by advocacy-oriented charities such as NBUF; these regulations were eventually ruled illegal by an appellate court (National Committee for Responsive Philanthropy, 1989, n.d.; Anderson, 1977). Today, while alternative funds can now enjoy the benefit of access to CFC, few, if any, bear the scars of and the burden of the continuing ill will that continues to be directed toward NBUF as a result of its leadership role in this area.

Second battlefront: Private workplace campaigns

NBUF also helped to pioneer methods for obtaining access to the charitable campaigns of private employers, and, again, these efforts reinforced the movement nature of the organization, generated animosity from United Way's corporate supporters, and raised the question of black separatism. To gain campaign access among private employers, NBUF developed a strategy of relying on the firms' black workers to lobby on its behalf (Douglas, 1982, p. 4). At New Jersey's Bell Laboratories, for example, in 1979, several hundred employees petitioned the company to allow the New Jersey BUF into the campaign. The company initially rejected the petition but changed its mind in 1981 when Kenneth Clark, a noted black psychologist, completed a study recommending that the fund be let in on a trial basis. In 1983, the New Jersey BUF finally gained permanent access at the Bell Laboratories site (Amamoo, 1984). A similar strategy was used to gain access to IBM sites in New York and New Jersey (National Committee for Responsive Philanthropy, 1986, pp. 17–21).

NBUF's leadership on the CFC issue, coupled with its approach of actively organizing the black employees of private employers to lobby company executives to allow local BUFs to participate in private workplace campaigns, did little to endear NBUF to United Way or its corporate supporters. Moreover, NBUF's use of explicit racial appeals may have indirectly laid the groundwork for the subsequent development of other black charitable federations. For example, Associated Black Charities in Baltimore and New York were created with the financial support of United Way, and their affiliates are full participating members of their local United Way organizations (Berkley, 1992).

Conclusion

In *Profiles of Excellence: Achieving Success in the Nonprofit Sector,* the authors state that there are four hallmarks of an effective nonprofit organization: primacy of mission, effective leadership, a dynamic board, and strong fundraising development programs (Knauft, Berger, and Gray, 1991, pp. 1–2). This chapter has demonstrated that in the early years of its development, NBUF exhibited all of these traits. More specifically, NBUF's twofold mission was clear, Walter Bremond was an extraordinary leader, the board represented a diversity of ideological perspectives and constituencies, and the organization had developed important relationships with several foundations, none more important than the Cummins Engine Foundation, which provided long-term financial and in-kind support. In addition,

NBUF's success in pursuing access to CFC and the work-site charitable campaigns of private employers further diversified NBUF's funding base.

The difficulty in discussing any aspect of NBUF, no matter how narrowly defined, is that it is a complex institution that has grappled with a number of difficult issues. From one perspective, it is a fascinating testimony to NBUF's founders—in particular, Walter Bremond—that they envisioned and, for a time, sustained a movement for social change and built local BUFs to serve as social change charitable organizations. However, NBUF's dual mission made continued long-term success on both issues unlikely for a number of reasons.

Social movements are difficult to start and often grow out of a confluence of circumstances. Moreover, once started, social movements are difficult to sustain as circumstances change and key individuals go on to other pursuits. In hindsight, it is not surprising that the local BUFs wanted, as they grew stronger, to exert more control over NBUF. After all, NBUF is a federation of members to which it is ultimately responsible. To the extent that some local BUFs began to see themselves as black versions of United Way rather than as local agents of social change, one of two things became inevitable: either local BUFs would withdraw from NBUF because it was not serving their interests, or NBUF would begin to focus on the needs of local BUFs, as it has done. In this setting, the non-BUF-affiliated board members never gained sufficient organizational standing to challenge their counterparts representing local BUFs.

Although less prominent than in the past, NBUF continues to play a leadership role in the alternative fund movement. For example, it continues to expand access to work-site charitable payroll deduction plans to nontraditional charities. In addition, William Merritt, NBUF's current executive director, has launched a new organization, the National Black United Federation of Charities, consisting of a cross section of black organizations under NBUF's leadership, with the goal of directing an even larger percentage of charitable dollars toward black causes. With these events, NBUF continues its proud tradition of advocating black self-determination through the development of black fundraising organizations to support black institutions.

References

Amamoo, J. "Black United Fund: A Notion of Self-Investment." *Focus*, Aug.-Sept. 1984, pp. 34–35.

Anderson, L. K. "The Federal Government and Black Fund Raising." *Black Scholar*, Dec. 1977, pp. 12–20.

Bakewell, D.J.X. "The Brotherhood Crusade: A Conceptual Model." *Black Scholar*, Mar. 1976, pp. 22–26.

Berkley, R. "Different Philosophies of Caring: The Relationship Between the Black United Fund, the Associated Black Charities and New York City's Black Community, 1979–1989." Paper presented at the conference Philanthropy and Cultural Diversity, Center for the Study of Philanthropy, City University of New York, June 1992.

Bothwell, R. O., and Saasta, T. "Walter Bremond: A Social Activist with a Vision." *Grantsmanship Center News*, July-Aug. 1982, pp. 65–67.

Bremond, W. "The National Black United Fund Movement." *Black Scholar*, Mar. 1976, pp. 10–15.

Bremond, W. "United Way Monopoly: Its Legal and Political Aspects and What It Means to Exclude Black Organizations." Address presented at the conference Fund-Raising in the Workplace: Exploring Alternatives to United Way, Dallas, April 1978.

Bryce, H. J. *Financial and Strategic Management for Nonprofit Organizations.* Englewood Cliffs, N.J.: Prentice Hall, 1992.

Carson, E. D. *The Attitudes, Accessibility, and Participation of Blacks and Whites in Work-Site Charitable Payroll Deduction Plans.* Durham, N.C.: Center for the Study of Philanthropy and Voluntarism, Duke University, 1988.

Carson, E. D. "The Evolution of Black Philanthropy: Patterns of Giving and Voluntarism." In R. Magat (ed.), *Philanthropic Giving: Studies in Varieties and Goals.* New York: Oxford University Press, 1989.

Carson, E. D. "Contemporary Trends in Black Philanthropy: Challenging the Myths." In D. F. Burlingame and L. J. Hulse (eds.), *Taking Fund Raising Seriously: Advancing the Profession and Practice of Raising Money.* San Francisco: Jossey-Bass, 1991.

Carson, E. D. *A Hand Up: Black Philanthropy and Self-Help in America.* Washington, D.C.: Joint Center for Political and Economic Studies, 1993.

Davis, K. E. *Fund Raising in the Black Community.* Metuchen, N.J.: Scarecrow Press, 1975.

Davis, K. E. "The National Black United Fund: Self-Help for Black People." Unpublished manuscript, 1982.

Douglas, P. "Black United Fund Chips Away at White Charity Establishment." *National Leader*, Dec. 9, 1982, pp. 1–4.

Drucker, P. F. *Managing the Nonprofit Organization.* New York: HarperCollins, 1990.

Griffin, B. "National Black United Fund Second Annual Conference: A Retrospective." *Black Scholar*, July-Aug. 1978, pp. 48–49.

Hodgkinson, V. A., Weitzman, M. S., Toppe, C. M., and Noga, S. M. (eds.). *Nonprofit Almanac 1992–93: Dimensions of the Independent Sector.* San Francisco: Jossey-Bass, 1992.

Jenkins, P. "The Black United Fund Movement: An Interview with Walter Bremond and James Joseph." *Grantsmanship Center News*, 1977, pp. 20–28.

Joseph, J. A. "Philanthropy and the Black Economic Condition." *Black Scholar*, Mar. 1976, pp. 5–9.

Knauft, E. B., Berger, R. A., and Gray, S. T. *Profiles of Excellence: Achieving Success in the Nonprofit Sector.* San Francisco: Jossey-Bass, 1991.

National Committee for Responsive Philanthropy. *The Combined Federal Campaign: A Special Report.* Washington, D.C.: National Committee for Responsive Philanthropy, n.d.

National Committee for Responsive Philanthropy. "Many Companies Decide That United Way Is Not the Only Way." In *Charity Begins at Work.* Washington, D.C.: National Committee for Responsive Philanthropy, 1986.

National Committee for Responsive Philanthropy. *Special Report on Workplace Giving: The New Era.* Washington, D.C.: National Committee for Responsive Philanthropy, 1989.

Palmer, E. "The United Way and the Black Community in Atlanta, Georgia." *Black Scholar*, Dec. 1977, pp. 50–61.

Polivy, D. K. *Increasing Giving Options in Corporate Charitable Payroll Deduction Programs: Who Benefits?* New Haven, Conn.: Program on Nonprofit Organizations, Yale University, 1985.

"United Black Fund: A Vital New Vehicle for Blacks to Begin Leading Blacks." *National Black Monitor*, 1984, *9* (9), 7–15.

Witty, C. J. *Employee Attitudes, Perceptions, and Behavior.* Working Paper No. 9. San Francisco: Institute for Nonprofit Organizational Management, University of San Francisco, 1989.

EMMETT D. CARSON *is program officer in the Governance and Public Policy Program at the Ford Foundation in New York and a scholar on philanthropy.*

This chapter details the birth, early development, and fundraising strategies of the American Indian College Fund, incorporated in 1987 as a tax-exempt nonprofit organization to raise funds from the private sector to advance American Indian higher education. The fund is unique in its support for the American Indian tribal colleges, which are located primarily on Indian reservations across the United States.

5

"The future is in our minds": The American Indian College Fund

Ronald Austin Wells

From idea to reality

Like so many other organizations, the American Indian College Fund began as an idea formed in the crucible of necessity. That necessity arose from the cumulative failures of this nation to provide adequate systems of education to meet the needs of American Indians, particularly those living on reservations. In this chapter, I do not detail the difficult history of Native American peoples, except to note that this American minority has suffered greatly at the hands of the majority society, with inadequate education at the center of that tragic history.

NEW DIRECTIONS FOR PHILANTHROPIC FUNDRAISING, NO. 1, FALL 1993 © JOSSEY-BASS PUBLISHERS

The formation of the American Indian College Fund can best be understood within a more immediate historical context, which begins when the first tribal colleges were established on American Indian reservations. Recognizing that the education system of the majority culture was not satisfactory, American Indian leaders had for many years discussed establishing their own schools and colleges. In 1968, the Navajo nation in northern Arizona granted a charter to Navajo Community College to establish a campus at Many Farms (now Tsaile) on the Navajo reservation. Three years later, the Oglala Sioux tribe at Pine Ridge reservation in South Dakota chartered Oglala Sioux Community College (now Oglala Lakota College), and the Rosebud Sioux tribe chartered Sinte Gleska College. In 1972, three more institutions joined the ranks, and, by 1978, the number of tribal colleges on Indian reservations had increased to over twenty.

The United States Congress passed the Tribal Community Colleges Act of 1978, giving federal authorization for the establishment of two-year community colleges on American Indian reservations. Like virtually everything else that has had to do with the federally controlled destiny of the American Indian, the colleges—and their funding—were placed under the purview of the Bureau of Indian Affairs, with funding dependent on annual Congressional appropriations for the Department of the Interior. Although a certain minimal level of funding (based on full-time-equivalent enrollment of Indian students) was thereby established, appropriations and funding formulas never have approached levels adequate to meet the colleges' needs. The historically difficult and painful relationship between American Indians and the Bureau of Indian Affairs is well known; suffice it to say that partly because of the unpredictable vagaries and vicissitudes of the Congress and the executive branch, the leaders of the tribal colleges from the very beginning identified the lack of adequate financial resources as their number one problem (Carnegie Foundation for the Advancement of Teaching, 1989, p. 35).

In 1973, these leaders, the presidents of the tribal colleges, established the American Indian Higher Education Consortium (AIHEC), with the purpose of sharing ideas, knowledge, and resources to advance the tribal college movement. The president of each tribally chartered college had a seat on the AIHEC board, which elected its own officers annually. Representatives from Indian nations such as the Lakota Sioux, Navajo, Chippewa, and Hidatsa—some, former ancient enemies—came together in this common cause (Stein, 1990, p. 18).

It was clear to the leaders of this new movement in American Indian higher education that the federal funding for the colleges was pitifully inadequate to the task that lay before them: to deliver higher education, and hence economic opportunity, to Native American populations on the reservations. These presidents, almost all of whom were American Indians who had received their educations at "mainstream" institutions, understood that if the tribal colleges were ever to thrive or, indeed, survive, some means must be found of attracting funding from private sources. Some of the individual colleges had embarked on campaigns to raise their own funds from corporate and other private sources, but with little success; the geographical isolation of most of the colleges, with virtually no corporations and few businesses on or near the reservations, as well as the economic and cultural distance from white America, proved to be formidable obstacles to raising significant private funds. As they met to discuss common problems, the presidents realized that attempts to raise private sector funds for a single college would be ineffective. To compete with each other for extremely limited resources, furthermore, would be self-defeating; to do so was also inconsistent with American Indian values, which set a higher value on the good of the community, or group, than on the good of any individual member (Deloria, 1970, p. 136).

The presidents also discussed the possibility of hiring a professional fundraiser to work on behalf of all of the colleges together. In those earliest years in the development of the tribal colleges, the idea of a collective fund, such as the United Negro College Fund, accruing to the benefit of all was advanced by several of the leaders of these new, developing institutions: David Gipp and Perry Horse of the AIHEC staff; Dean Jackson, Navajo Community College; and James Shanley, Fort Peck Community College, were all early advocates.

Creation of the American Indian College Fund

At a conference in Missoula, Montana, in 1985, the members of AIHEC's board proposed to undertake a serious effort to raise funds in the private sector. As an internal memorandum put it, "1985 marked the initial year of AIHEC's commitment to embark on a total fundraising effort." At the meeting, the AIHEC board invited three individuals to join them in this effort: Vito Perrone, an educator; Rose Robinson, a member of the Hopi tribe and a national activist in Native American issues; and Anne Sward Hansen, a television actress. A former dean of higher education at the University of North Dakota and a trusted friend and adviser to Indian education, Perrone had helped establish tribal colleges at Turtle Mountain and Standing Rock in North Dakota and had served as a consultant on Indian issues to the governor of North Dakota. Robinson was vice president of American Indian affairs in the Washington, D.C., office of the Phelps-Stokes Fund, a foundation with a charter mandate in American Indian education. Hansen, a professional singer and actress on the New York-based daytime television drama "As the World Turns," had been involved in charitable activities related to American Indian children. Learning of Sinte Gleska College during a visit to the Rosebud Sioux reservation in South Dakota, and comprehending that here was a practical, viable way to attack the poverty on Indian reservations, Hansen offered to help raise funds for the colleges.

These three individuals had been invited to sit in on the meeting of the AIHEC board to discuss the new fundraising initiative. Among the college presidents, there had been some disagreement as to the form, that is, the guiding principles and the rules of governance, that the American Indian College Fund should take. Most of the presidents acknowledged the need for establishing a permanent endowment to ensure the financial stability of the colleges. Most accepted the need to engage outside expertise (specifically, a professional fundraiser) not readily available on the reservations. Recognizing the common purpose and cause of the tribal colleges, most affirmed a transcendent national vision. Some, however, were concerned that a separate college fund would compete with the colleges for funds. Some, understandably apprehensive, argued that if the AIHEC board did not maintain control, the enterprise could be exploited by others and not work directly to the benefit of the Indian colleges. From their perspective, the American Indian College Fund, therefore, would have to remain a subsidiary function of AIHEC. Others, citing the example of the United Negro College Fund, argued that the activity would achieve greater success raising funds as a separate entity. What was essential, all recognized, was to "go where the money is": The fundraising efforts had to be focused, first, in the East (particularly New York City), and then in other urban centers where both corporate and private donors were likely to be found, such as San Francisco and Minneapolis.

The day following the meeting, the president of the AIHEC board, Joseph McDonald of Salish-Kootenai College, invited Perrone, Robinson, and Hansen to form a steering committee for the establishment of the American Indian College Fund. Those three, and the executive committee of the AIHEC board—four officers and two at-large members, all presidents of tribal institutions—would form the first working board. The principle of Indian (AIHEC) control was thereby ensured. The fund, which would be separately incorporated with its own tax-exempt status, would embark on fundraising and public relations activities in New York City with volunteers under Hansen's leadership. Its objective would be to raise endowment and thus not compete with the colleges for program funds. A formal mission statement and bylaws would be drafted; for the time being, however, the mandate was clear: Raise money from the private sector to help the tribal colleges.

Accessing the philanthropic community

As these developments were unfolding, AIHEC's congressional liaison and acting executive director, John Forkenbrock, and an independent consultant, Tod Bedrosian, had been working in Washington, D.C., on behalf of the tribal college consortium. Bedrosian, for instance, organized a fundraising dinner at which Senator Daniel K. Inouye, chairman of the Senate Select Committee on Indian Affairs, was honored for his leadership on issues affecting American Indians; that dinner also served as a forum to announce the establishment of the American Indian College Fund to the press and general public. To seed the fundraising effort, AIHEC authorized $5,000 from its own treasury to underwrite a development plan. The first step was to begin making contacts with foundations and corporations who could be potential funders.

Aware of her reputation for providing technical assistance in fundraising to American Indian groups, Forkenbrock had been in contact with Rose Robinson of the Phelps-Stokes Fund. An operating foundation with a long and distinguished history of aiding Indian causes, reaching back to its support of Meriam's (1928) pathbreaking study, *The Problem of Indian Administration* (commonly known as the "Meriam Report"), the Phelps-Stokes Fund was well positioned to provide access to the philanthropic community. At that time, Robinson, well known in Indian country for her work with grass-roots and national Indian organizations, was making final plans for a two-day series of meetings with grantmaking foundations in New York for Indian groups. She invited AIHEC to participate.

In November 1985, Robinson's efforts brought representatives of approximately a dozen Indian organizations and a like number of grantmakers together at the Rockefeller and Ford foundations for the two-day conference American Indian Education Today. The presentations at Rockefeller by Janine Pease Windy Boy, president of Little Big Horn College at Crow Agency, Montana, and at Ford, the following day, by Sherman Marshall of Sinte Gleska College established or reinforced contact between the Indian colleges and several of the grantmaking foundations. While no subsequent grants resulted directly from these meetings, the presentations greatly raised awareness of the colleges and their funding needs in the New York philanthropic community.

Another meeting, held in 1988 after the American Indian College Fund had been incorporated, achieved the long-needed breakthrough in funding. Having committed itself to the success of the enterprise, the Phelps-Stokes Fund sponsored a luncheon atop the corporate headquarters of McGraw-Hill in New York City, with the purpose of bringing the American Indian College Fund to the attention of New York grantmaking foundations. Through AIHEC, the fund invited all of the tribal colleges to send representatives; nineteen of the college presidents made their way to New York to attend the luncheon. To ensure attendance of funders, the Phelps-Stokes executive vice president sent personal letters to the heads of more than fifty grantmaking foundations, inviting them to a luncheon presentation where the American Indian College Fund project would be launched and where they would have the opportunity to meet these distinguished leaders in American Indian higher education. In follow-up telephone calls, he reinforced the personal nature of the invitation, expressing enthusiasm for the potential of the tribal colleges and promising that the meeting would last no longer than two hours. Representatives of more than a dozen foundations accepted the invitation.

At the luncheon, at least two college presidents were seated at each of the circular tables of six, thus affording the opportunity to talk at length about his or her own school, the students, and the challenges and promise that higher education brought to the reservations. The lunch was light, appetizing, and quickly served. With coffee, Phelps-Stokes's executive vice president introduced the formal presentations. For American Indians, he said, the road to equality of opportunity has been tortuous, strewn with the broken promises of the United States government. Under the most difficult conditions, the tribal colleges have proved themselves durable and worthy institutions offering great hope for the future of American Indians.

Now the American Indian College Fund was a reality, offering grant-making foundations an opportunity to access Indian institutions in an effective and powerful way. And here was their story.

Anne Sward Hansen, chairperson of the fund's board, then narrated a slide presentation to provide an overview of the colleges. The slides showed a wooden-frame building, standing alone on the stark South Dakota plain; a computer class, held in a converted gymnasium; an Indian student, placing the eagle feather on her nurse's cap at graduation as she was congratulated by her grandmother in traditional Indian dress. Actress Hansen's narrative, punctuated by her dramatic asides describing the students and teachers encountered during her visits to the colleges, enthralled the audience. Two presidents followed: Lionel Bordeaux, an imposing six feet three inches tall, president since 1972 of Sinte Gleska College at Rosebud Sioux, spoke forcefully about the beginnings of the colleges, the struggles to survive, and the indomitable will to succeed as American Indian institutions. Janine Pease Windy Boy, striking with her long dark hair in braids, described with soft-spoken eloquence Little Big Horn College at Crow Agency, Montana, where, in addition to serving as president, she taught classes in English composition to students whose first language was Crow. She told the audience of how the school had started in an old gymnasium. She talked about the students at her school—an average age of thirty-four, more than two-thirds women, who routinely drove many miles through fierce snowstorms to get to class. She told about Crow traditions, of their reverence for nature and family, and of the graduate of Little Big Horn College who went on to complete her bachelor's and master's degrees at Montana State University and was the first geologist in the Crow tribe.

Then, according to plan, the host called on each of the tribal college presidents in turn. Standing at their tables, the presidents introduced themselves and their schools, one after another; their commitment, competence, and quiet, reasoned style were impressive. The meeting adjourned within the promised two hours in a spirit of shared joy and promise.

That luncheon meeting led directly to the first major administrative funding for the American Indian College Fund. The Lilly Endowment invited a proposal for a seed grant. The Exxon Education Foundation also said that it would entertain a proposal. The U.S. West Foundation, with whom discussions had already begun, reaffirmed an interest in providing funding. Subsequent follow-up garnered administrative support from the Pew Memorial Trusts and endowment challenge grants from the MacArthur and Hearst foundations. This early support pledged nearly $500,000 over three years to get the fund up and running, allowing the board to begin the process of putting paid professional staff in place.

Board's role: Mission, bylaws, and policy setting

The founding board of the American Indian College Fund comprised the three original incorporators (Hansen, Perrone, and Robinson) and, ex officio, the executive committee of AIHEC, that is, those college presidents who were serving as officers of the consortium. Later, other prominent individuals, such as Ben Nighthorse Campbell (D-Colo.), the only American Indian serving in the United States Congress, were invited to join the board.

As these individuals came together in their first meetings, they encountered the responsibilities and challenges confronting every new organization. Since, in this instance, the organization had been created to address a specific need, the task of drafting the mission statement was a reasonably straightforward process. After some discussion and several revisions, the board approved its statement of mission: "to raise funds from the private sector to provide scholarship aid and developmental assistance to the member institutions of the American Indian Higher Education Consortium, . . . compris[ing] the tribally chartered American Indian colleges, which are located primarily on Indian reservations across the United States" (American Indian College Fund, 1991, p. 1). All of the members of the board agreed that the singular focus of the mission was an advantage and strength. Even though the general public as yet knew little about the tribal colleges, the mission and objectives of the fund would be easy to understand.

At its second meeting, held in 1988, the board approved the fund's bylaws, prepared by a committee chaired by James Shanley. These included the usual areas of trustee responsibility: methods of appointment and removal of members, officers, meetings, and terms of office. The bylaws authorized a board of up to fifteen members and specified that a plurality would be presidents of member colleges. Along with the normal fiduciary responsibility, the bylaws established the authority of the board "to distribute assets and funds to the member colleges"; the bylaws did not include, however, any specific policy statement on how that distribution should be made.

Financial management and distribution policy

In order to mount an effective fundraising campaign, every organization, new or well established, must present an image of sound and reliable fiscal management and stability. In the case of the American Indian College Fund, an additional cultural dimension complicated this issue. In the collective American psyche, romanticized images of the American Indian (Geronimo, Uncas, Cochise) coexist, paradoxically, with negative stereotypes of Indians. As with most prejudice, however, such stereotypes cannot stand up to the reality of human interaction. Once donors were given the opportunity to meet with Indian leaders, any such stereotypes, if they existed, were dispelled, and mutual trust and confidence were established.

The success of the American Indian College Fund in attracting initial administrative support was also due in part to its affiliation with a well-established organization, the Phelps-Stokes Fund. Under the leadership of its president, Franklin H. Williams, Phelps-Stokes had undertaken the task of helping to create or develop new organizations that would advance its own mission: educational opportunity for American minorities. The mission of the college fund was a perfect match, and the venerable foundation took the fledgling newcomer under its wing. In addition to offering office space and technical assistance in development, the Phelps-Stokes Fund was able to provide expenditure responsibility for the first administrative grants. Phelps-Stokes thereby gave the American Indian College Fund an added credibility to grantmakers and reduced, in their eyes, the sense of risk that often accompanies the funding of a new organization. Even more significant for attracting funding, however, was the nature of the cause and the eloquence of its spokespersons. Increased educational opportunity for American Indians was an unassailable goal. By successfully struggling against great odds, the tribally chartered colleges had proved themselves viable and durable institutions. And the pride and determination of the Indian leaders were inspirational.

Knowing that it was the key to long-range stability, the board moved immediately to build a permanent endowment. An early decision set the pattern: The modest sum of approximately $5,000 was approved for investment with a professional manager to establish the endowment fund. Challenge grants (one dollar match for every two dollars raised) from the John D. and Catherine T. MacArthur Foundation and the William Randolph Hearst Foundation provided additional incentive to add to the endowment as quickly as possible. With confidence in its vision, the board announced its goal: a permanent endowment of $10 million by 1992.

Well before any significant funds had been raised, the first question asked by potential donors was, of course, "How will the money be used?" Even before the college fund initiative had begun, the presidents of the twenty-six tribal colleges had discussed and debated the question of the distribution of funds. Once money started coming in, how would it be handled? What share would each college get? On the one hand, it seemed to make sense to divide funds proportionately to the size of each institution: Logically, should not the college with one thousand students get a larger share than the college with three hundred? But who can say that the latter, because of its small size, does not need the support all the more? Another suggestion was to make the distribution of funds competitive among the colleges, with the best proposals winning the grants. But none of these opinions was persuasive. The only formula acceptable to all was equal distribution to each college. As board chairperson Hansen observed, "Only that [option] is consistent with 'Indian way'—sharing resources equally regardless of how limited they may be."

Once the college fund's own board was established, the question was revisited, with the board unanimously affirming the policy of equal distribution of income. In 1988, even though relatively little money had been raised, the fund moved to approve its first distribution. It was important, the board felt, to establish this precedent for both operational and symbolic reasons. First, the need for scholarships and other support was so great; how, Lionel Bordeaux asked passionately at one meeting, could he explain to his students at Sinte Gleska that the fund's board was holding back on much-needed scholarship funds? Second, members of the board felt that it was important to demonstrate their commitment to the colleges in real terms. Thus, barely a year after the fund's incorporation, the board approved grants-in-aid of $800 to each of the member colleges for student scholarships, for a total distribution of just over $20,000. While this was a very modest amount, the distribution demonstrated that the college fund meant what it said, and that it existed to raise money for the colleges, not for itself. The decision enhanced trust and strengthened relationships with the individual colleges. One year later, fundraising efforts had been so successful that the board was able to increase its distribution by greater than a factor of ten, awarding $10,000 in scholarship funds to each member institution, for a total of $260,000 in 1990. That amount was repeated in 1991, and redoubled in 1992, with grants to each college of $20,000, for a total of $520,000.

Special events policy

Another problem that the American Indian College Fund encountered was the need to establish a mechanism of control over volunteer efforts. As members of the board recruited volunteer talent to help with various fundraising projects and the fund began to become known, creative and enthusiastic individuals came forward with one project after another, such as benefit dinners and concerts. It quickly became clear that since the final responsibility for any activity using the college fund's name lay with the board, some form of control of special events was an absolute necessity.

In crafting its policy statement, the board defined a special event as one "outside the scope of normal fundraising activities" (such as direct-mail or corporate giving campaigns). It established a committee on special events with the authority to review all plans for fundraising benefits. A sponsoring group was required to submit a formal proposal that described the type of event, target audience, responsible volunteer personnel, project budget, and anticipated revenues. The board would review such proposals once a year, prior to drafting its annual plan. Once in place, this policy helped improve planning and coordination and brought special events directly under the board's control.

Putting staff in place

With three-year administrative support secured, the American Indian College Fund moved to its next phase of development: putting the first professional staff into place. After discussing at length job specifications and qualifications for an executive director, the board appointed a search committee. While an American Indian director was highly desirable, the most important qualification, as Lionel Bordeaux put it, was "someone who could raise money." At this early stage of its development, the college fund needed a self-starter and a quick study, a person with both a track record and the skill and imagination to take the fund to new heights.

In the summer of 1989, following a national search, the college fund appointed as its first acting director Barbara Bratone. A professional fundraiser who had successfully worked with various minority organizations in New York City, Bratone was also familiar with the tribal college movement. She had impressive experience with corporate campaigns, direct-mail solicitation, and special events. And she brought an unbounded store of energy to the task.

Bratone took on every aspect of organizational development. She worked with the board to refine the development plan, to enhance the committee structure, and to improve internal communications. She worked with individual board members and numerous other volunteers to put on special events. She visited the tribal colleges and worked closely with their presidents. She engaged public relations people to design, pro bono, public service announcements, video promotions, and a logo for the fund. She mounted a vigorous and effective effort to attract corporate contributions. And she initiated and test-marketed a direct-mail campaign whose returns gave unprecedented results. When that campaign entered its second phase, it carried a letter written by Janine Pease Windy Boy, inviting the American people to become honorary alumni of the tribal colleges: "Tribal colleges are finally breaking the educational and economic isolation of America's forgotten Indian reservations. . . . After 500 years, Indian people again have hope—hope founded in effective educational opportunity. But there is one fact that we cannot overcome by ourselves. As America's newest colleges serving America's poorest people, we have no alumni we can turn to for financial support. However, with your sustained support and the participation of new friends, we can change the odds against Indian people forever" (American Indian College Fund, 1991, p. 1). By 1990, with Bratone's strong direction, the American Indian College Fund was on the American philanthropic map.

Public relations, special events, and volunteers

Special fundraising events proved to be an effective method of rallying volunteers to the cause of the American Indian College Fund. One such project proposed to hold a benefit auction of American Indian art at a prestigious gallery in New York City. Not only would this create a glamorous special event (in New York parlance, a "gala," of which there are hundreds each year in Manhattan alone) to raise money for the college fund, but also, by creating a venue for their work, the project would give American Indian artists exposure in New York markets. In addition to the rewards of working for an important and compelling cause, the project offered volunteers access to three worlds: the world of art and artists, the world of New York society, and the world of the American Indian, made tangible for New Yorkers through the work of prominent American Indian artists and craftspersons. Board chairperson Hansen gathered friends and contacts from television, advertising, and art galleries. Among them was Gail Bruce, who owned her own gallery and whose store of ideas and energy was limitless. Another was Reuben Silverbird, a Navajo who owned and operated Silverbird, the only American Indian restaurant in New York City.

The project committee called on the directors of the prestigious New York auction houses of Christie's, Sotheby's, and Phillips to solicit their sponsorship. With the approval of the college fund board, the committee hired a publicist, who began forming an honorary advisory committee: first, well-known American Indian artists, such as Amado Peña, Jaune Quick-to-See Smith, Allen Houser, and Kevin Red Star; and then celebrities who agreed to lend their name recognition to the effort, such as Tom Brokaw, Michael Douglas, Halston, David Hockney, Dustin Hoffman, Bianca Jagger, Burt Reynolds, and Maria Tallchief. Because they served as magnets to attract many others to the cause, the enlistment of these public personalities helped to create a pool of individuals who later also became donors to the college fund.

Under Hansen's leadership, members of the committee set out to the Indian Market, held annually in Sante Fe, New Mexico, in August, to solicit donations of artworks for the college fund benefit. They visited gallery receptions, which featured new work by Indian artists—paintings, sculptures, pottery, and jewelry. They asked gallery owners (who, after all, were thriving because of the work of American Indian artists) for ten minutes to speak publicly about the American Indian College Fund. They distributed brochures describing the fundraising project and asked individual artists to donate a work for a benefit auction in New York. Hansen and Congressman Ben Nighthorse Campbell (a skilled artist and silversmith himself) walked the great plaza in the center of town, talking up the college fund and the proposed auction to all who would listen. Hansen and Dean Jackson, president of Navajo Community College, spoke on local radio and television talk shows and appeared at a press conference with Sante Fe's mayor, Sam Pick. In three days of whirlwind activity, the Sante Fe arts community and the American Indian College Fund became partners in supporting American Indian higher education.

As with so many ambitious projects, the benefit auction was not without its problems. Communications with galleries and with individual artists were complex and often difficult. Logistical problems were daunting. At one point, when the director of the cooperating auction house resigned and the project was without a home, the planning committee scaled back. The result was a sale of American Indian art, craft, and jewelry, held in December 1988 in conjunction with a recognition awards dinner, in Gail and Murray Bruce's splendid loft overlooking downtown Manhattan and the Hudson River. In addition to netting several thousands of dollars for scholarships at the tribal colleges, the gala event won many new friends and supporters for the college fund.

A year later, another special benefit event capitalized on the momentum generated by the first. During approximately the same period that the American Indian College Fund had been developing, another Indian group's star had also been rising. By 1989, the American Indian Dance Theatre had begun to receive international recognition for its unique presentation by brilliant young Indian dancers of traditional dance forms in dynamic contemporary settings. The dance company had completed a national tour with a well-reviewed performance in Washington, D.C., and had been sent abroad under the auspices of the State Department's cultural exchange program. In conjunction with their forthcoming New York premiere, the company's executive producer, Barbara Schwei, offered to put on a benefit performance for the college fund. A volunteer committee, working with publicist C. C. Goldwater, began planning: corporate and individual sponsors, ticket sales, a benefit dinner to follow the performance. Since the dinner would have a southwestern theme, Goldwater asked Brendan Walsh of one of New York City's top southwestern restaurants, Arizona 206, to volunteer his talents. The result was remarkable, even for New York: roast squash soup, chili-rubbed free range chicken, and blue-corn bread. For decorations, the committee asked individual artists to erect twenty-foot-high papier-mâché totems, creating a stunning environment; on the tables were arrangements of ceremonial herbs, such as fresh juniper and sage, brought in from a dozen Indian reservations. Not only was the event successful in raising scholarship funds, but the premiere performance of the American Indian Dance Theatre, the menu and decor of the benefit dinner, and the American Indian College Fund received glowing notices in the next day's *New York Times* and *San Francisco Chronicle*, bringing the fund substantial national publicity.

Other special events followed. At Adelphi University on Long Island, pop singer DeeDee Kelly gave a benefit summer concert, and the designer Mary McFadden dedicated a fashion show of her latest clothing to the benefit of the fund. In 1989, a Philadelphia-based benefit committee, under the formidable leadership of Christine Stainton, a prominent Philadelphian, sponsored its own successful corporate dinner.

These fundraising initiatives, generated primarily by volunteers, have repeatedly proved their value in funds and publicity. In each instance, the synergy of an attractive cause, enthusiastic and experienced volunteer committees, solid staff backup and board guidance have successfully raised funds for the tribal colleges.

Raising public awareness

As the time for the 1991 Academy Awards drew near, the director of the American Indian College Fund, Barbara Bratone, had a hunch.

Kevin Costner's film *Dances With Wolves* had received high praise for its sympathetic and sensitive portrayal of the Lakota people and nearly a dozen Academy Award nominations. To capitalize on the positive environment for American Indians that Costner's film was creating, Bratone wanted to place a full-page advertisement for the college fund in the *New York Times*. While she could not be certain that the film would win an Oscar, the opportunity to create an association of ideas seemed too good to pass up. After consulting with members of the board and gaining their approval, Bratone bought a full-page advertisement in the *Times* for the morning following the Academy Awards ceremony.

With its usual clarity, the *New York Times* reported on the seven Oscars that *Dances With Wolves* received. Unfortunately, however, the college fund advertisement did not appear in that edition. Early that morning, an angry Bratone appeared in the *Times* editorial office. Apologizing profusely, the embarrassed *Times* editor promised to run the advertisement the next day, at a reduced rate. As promised, the advertisement appeared, in the first section. It portrayed a beautiful American Indian woman in traditional Indian dress. At the top of the page, the text read, "The Past Is in Our Hearts—The Future Is in Our Minds"; at the bottom, simply, "The American Indian College Fund," along with an 800 toll-free number to call for pledges of contributions. The toll-free number received over four hundred calls that day from people pledging support, raising funds well in excess of the cost of the advertisement and giving the fund significant exposure at the national level.

Year of the American Indian

The American Indian College Fund (1992) has recorded encouraging results: nearly $7 million raised and more than ten thousand individual donors. What were some of the principles undergirding this successful fundraising effort? Foremost, AIHEC, seeing the need to create a strong organizing committee and founding board,

drafted knowledgeable, dedicated, capable people. Attracting others to the cause, and putting talented staff in place, those founders
created and fostered a strong sense of mission. They set specific
fundraising goals and strategies and started an endowment almost
immediately. They recognized the wisdom of affiliating with a well-
known organization to gain credibility and access and understood the
importance of cultivating personal contacts with potential donors,
of building a broad constituency through public relations, and of
capitalizing on opportunities in the external environment, in this
case, rising interest in Native Americans. By following these principles, the American Indian College Fund became exactly what it
wanted to be: a player on the national stage of philanthropic and
charitable activity.

Recognizing the opportunity to harness the swirling energies of
the Columbian quincentenary and to emphasize the positive contributions of Native American culture, the fund's fundraising campaign shifted into high gear for 1992. To achieve highly visible Indian
leadership, the board asked David Archambault to accept the pres-
idency of the fund. Archambault, president of Standing Rock Community College in Fort Yates, North Dakota, agreed to take a two-year
leave to assume leadership of the fund and become the national
spokesman. With Bratone continuing as executive director, the fund
set out to expand its direct-mail campaign and engaged the pro bono
services of a major advertising firm. Fundraising materials strike the
theme "Help us save a culture that may help us save ours." Following a test mailing, the agency launched a major national campaign,
including full-page advertisements in major print media.

In March 1992, Home Box Office hosted a reception for the fund
in conjunction with the premiere of the television film *The Last of His
Tribe*, starring Graham Greene as Ishi, the lone survivor of the Yahi
tribe of California, who is "discovered" in 1911 by an anthropolo-
gist, played by Jon Voight. In recognition of their work advancing
the cause of American Indians, fund president Archambault presented Indian star quilts to Greene, Voight, and the producers before
an audience of six hundred people. It was a joyous evening. As

Archambault (1992) noted in his presentation, the forthcoming anniversary of Columbus's voyage was a time for reflection and healing. On the great American plains, the Big Foot Riders had retraced the journey to Wounded Knee and completed the "wiping of tears" ceremony, releasing the spirits of dead ancestors. In Washington, D.C., President Bush declared 1992 to be the Year of the American Indian. On more than twenty reservations, American Indians were enrolling at their colleges and then going on to further education and employment. And looking forward to the twenty-first century, the American Indian College Fund could see a horizon bright with promise.

References

American Indian College Fund. *Report for 1987–1990.* New York: American Indian College Fund, 1991.

American Indian College Fund. *Report for 1991.* New York: American Indian College Fund, 1992.

Archambault, D. "Columbus Plus 500 Years: Whither the American Indian?" *Vital Speeches of the Day,* 1992, *58* (16), 491–493.

Carnegie Foundation for the Advancement of Teaching. *Tribal Colleges: Shaping the Future of Native America.* Princeton, N.J.: Carnegie Foundation for the Advancement of Teaching, 1989.

Deloria, V., Jr. *We Talk, You Listen.* New York: Macmillan, 1970.

Meriam, L. *The Problem of Indian Administration.* Washington, D.C.: Institute of Government Research, 1928.

Stein, W. "Founding of the American Indian Higher Education Consortium." *Tribal College: Journal of American Indian Higher Education,* 1990, *2* (1), 18–22.

RONALD AUSTIN WELLS *is former executive vice president and currently scholar-in-residence at the Phelps-Stokes Fund in New York City and an independent consultant to grantmaking foundations. He is a member of the board of directors of the New York Regional Association of Grantmakers and a member of the Research Committee of INDEPENDENT SECTOR.*

Raising $7.8 million to build a controversial AIDS nursing facility in less than five years took an extraordinary mix of the right personalities, fortuitous timing, grass-roots support, crackerjack lawyers and grant proposal writers, connections with the business and political communities, carefully planned groundwork, and passion.

6

Bailey-Boushay House: Passion, politics, and the art of public-private fundraising

Stephen Silha

THE AIDS EPIDEMIC is like a series of time bombs, buried in people's front yards. Some have already exploded, ripping the fabric of personal and community lives. Aftershocks are rocking cities and towns around the world; people long to feel some power over this deadly disease.

It was that longing that propelled nearly six thousand individuals to give money, time, and creativity to help build the $7.8 million Bailey-Boushay House in Seattle, the first skilled nursing facility and day health program designed and built specifically for people with AIDS. But the project did not just happen.

NEW DIRECTIONS FOR PHILANTHROPIC FUNDRAISING, NO. 1, FALL 1993 © JOSSEY-BASS PUBLISHERS

Coordinated approach

Like other urban areas in the United States, Seattle and King County saw steadily mounting AIDS cases in 1987. Projections showed that by 1991 King County would have fifteen hundred people with AIDS; by 1995, five thousand. The epidemic was not going away. Unlike most urban areas, however, Seattle's health care system, strengthened by a model network of community clinics, was developing a coordinated response to the AIDS crisis. The Robert Wood Johnson Foundation had given a $1.2 million, four-year grant to the Seattle-King County Department of Public Health to handle the planning, organization, development, networking, research, and public relations that would be necessary to respond to the AIDS crisis in the most humane and cost-effective ways.

Betsy Lieberman is one of many people whose lives have unexpectedly been touched by AIDS. As clinic coordinator of the Pike Market Community Clinic in downtown Seattle, she saw gay men and intravenous drug users become sick—and some die—even before the virus had a name. But when one of her friends returned from a routine medical blood test with a positive reading on the Human Immunodeficiency Virus (HIV), it transferred the crisis from a professional to a personal arena. She quit her job and took six months off to travel and think. Then, she took a part-time job, funded by one small piece of the Robert Woods Johnson Foundation grant, planning for housing and long-term care needs of people with AIDS.

Pinpointing unmanageable costs

The need to find housing for people with AIDS had already been identified by the Seattle Mayor's AIDS Task Force. But the problem got more urgent as public and private medical systems began paying what then seemed exorbitant hospital costs of $600 to $800 a day for increasing numbers of AIDS patients. These patients needed skilled nursing care but could do just as well in nursing homes, where costs averaged $150 a day. The need for lower-cost care was clear.

Research and networking

Lieberman scoured King County nursing homes to see if they would accept people with AIDS. She found them already 98 percent full, and only one or two were willing to offer a bed or two for HIV-infected residents. Lieberman traveled to study what New York and San Francisco were doing to house their much greater numbers of people with AIDS. "Meeting with staff members and PWAs [people with AIDS] made me think more broadly," she said. "Hospice care wasn't enough" (personal communication, July 26, 1991; July 29, 1992).

Building a team

Lieberman convened an advisory planning committee of twenty-two health care and AIDS professionals. The committee included a chaplain, several hospital personnel, administrators from state, county, and city governments, housing experts, people with AIDS, social workers, academics, a researcher, nursing home operators, and the director of the Northwest AIDS Foundation, the nonprofit that played a key role in nurturing a growing network of nonprofits to provide direct services to AIDS patients and their families. The group met at 7:30 A.M. in the cafeteria of Seattle's Swedish Hospital every three weeks for seven months. Lieberman learned how to use busy people's time well, and to get diverse and sometimes competing agencies to work together. "It was absolutely critical to have representatives from the city, state, and county governments on the planning committee," she relates. "And it was amazing how people took to this project. We had 90 percent attendance."

Defining the response

The advisory planning committee made specific recommendations, which set the tone for the entire project: (1) development of a thirty-five-bedroom facility specializing in long-term care services for persons with AIDS; (2) flexibility in design so that residents have their own rooms and bathrooms and do not have to be moved when their care needs change, and incorporation of day/community space, congregate meal space, and an adult day health care center; (3) licensing as a skilled nursing facility, with state and insurance reimbursement rates specific to the complexity of care provided; (4) management by an experienced health care provider, working in partnership with a representative community board; (5) an environment accepting and affirming of residents' sexual orientations and relationships, spiritual or religious beliefs, and past histories of substance abuse; and (6) joint financing from federal, state, county, city, corporate, and private sources.

Timing is everything

As often happens in a project such as this, timing is everything. Just one week after the committee published its report and recommendations, the Health Resources and Services Administration (HRSA) of the U.S. Department of Health and Human Services/Public Health Service issued a request for proposals for the construction of long-term care facilities for people with AIDS.

All the months of planning and research paid off. The federal funding fit perfectly with what the committee proposed. But to apply for the federal money, Seattle needed to develop a nonprofit organization and come up with an elaborate proposal, including a preliminary design for the building—all in two months.

A local lawyer (and former aide to the late Senator Warren Magnuson) agreed to do the paperwork for the nonprofit organization; it needed a name, and he came up with AIDS Housing of Washington. A portion of the planning committee became the core board, but at this point it was clear that fundraising would be necessary. It was time to turn a program committee into a fundraising board. Easier said than done.

Key to the transformation was the involvement of such people as Shirley Bridge, a director of Ben Bridge Jewelers and longtime community activist. "This was a controversial project," Bridge remembers. "It had a stigma. People were hesitant" (personal communication, July 24, 1991). She brought to the board years of community contacts, and a long personal history in the medical field. For forty years she was a pharmacist, one of the first female pharmacists in the state of Washington. She helped start the Diabetes Research Center at the University of Washington; and as a board member of Harborview Hospital, she knew what was expected of boards. Since Bridge has cancer, she empathizes with people living with AIDS. "The AIDS and cancer viruses are no different," she says, "except one is more virulent." But equally important was that original planning committee members, including Donald Chamberlain, who managed the city's first AIDS hospice, and the Reverend Gwen Beighle, who mobilized the religious community around the AIDS issue, took leadership roles as fundraisers on the board.

Mission statement

At its founding meeting May 6, 1988, the new board approved a mission statement, based on the planning committee's recommendations, which guided all the board's activities. If there was ever a question about the project or the program, people went back to the mission statement for guidance.

The right leader

Lieberman, still working part-time on AIDS housing and part-time on a plan for the King County Division on Aging, realized that the new organization would need an executive director. Although other committee members told her that they thought she was the only person for the job, she had her doubts. "I'm not a developer," she said. "I'm a health care administrator." But she was the one who knew most about the need and the project. She had great contacts in the business and philanthropic communities from her work at the Pike Market Community Clinic. She had a knack for writing great proposals. And her zeal to follow through on the recommendations of the planning committee only strengthened as she watched more of her friends become ill. The county extended her contract to get the new organization off the ground, and the board hired her.

Lieberman continued preparing the proposal for the $500,000 grant from HRSA. She got architects to donate sketches and enlisted the partnership of the Sisters of Providence Health Care Corporation, whose long-term care staff helped to prepare the financial plans for the facility, and eventually to acquire the Certificate of Need and license to run a nursing home. She answered every question in detail, even if the answers were repetitive. She followed the grant proposal format to the letter. It was easy to get letters of support from planning committee members and others with whom she had spoken.

So now there was an organization, a director, and a board—but no money. The Northwest AIDS Foundation came through with a $2,000 loan to start the organization. Lieberman paid the rent and overhead for a few months with her own money as the organization grew into the office above the city's Pike Place Market that she had shared with another independent consultant. Board members chipped in.

Anonymous gift

And then, almost miraculously, an anonymous gift of $100,000 came in through the Catholic Archdiocese of Seattle. It kept the project alive. Organizers say they still do not know who donated the money. But it may have had something to do with the partnership with Sisters of Providence and the broad-based community networking that the board members began. Momentum grew; more proposals went out, and in the summer of 1988 the group began looking for a site. They considered renovating an existing nursing home but found that they could build a new facility for the same money and get better amenities such as parking.

Acquiring the site: Tweaking the vision

A site in the Madison Valley neighborhood at Twenty-Eighth Avenue East and East Madison Street, where Bailey-Boushay House stands today, seemed perfect. It had the right zoning. Nobody would have to be displaced; there were one abandoned house and five vacant lots. The lots had served as informal parking lots and a dump site, and before that a pharmacy had sat on the corner. And the price was right: about $450,000. Within a month, the fledgling organization had signed options to buy the lots. Washington Mutual Savings Bank and the Seattle Housing Authority agreed to loan the money; the city had been represented on the planning committee, and certain board members had high-level access to bank officials.

Meetings with potential funders

At the same time, Lieberman and board members began canvassing local grantmakers to see if they would be willing to chip in to help the project, which they then thought would require about $2.5 million more than they anticipated getting from the federal, state, county, and city governments. (In the end, the private tab came to $4.3 million; government funds totaled $3.5 million.) "We did this in lieu of a 'feasibility study,' usually conducted before a capital campaign," Lieberman remembers. "We told them what we were doing, and asked if they would consider a grant application the following year." It was a long process, requiring patience. Some grantmakers said yes, some no, some maybe. But it paid off.

"We realized that education was as important as anything," says Michele Hasson (personal communication, July 19, 1991; July 30, 1992), who was hired later that year as the project's full-time fund developer. Her background as a solicitation trainer with the United Jewish Appeal entailed ample lessons in how to motivate people to help out, a key to any fundraising. During one of her first days on the job, she trekked to the Seattle Public Library's Foundation Center collections to look up potential funding sources. She eventually sent letters of inquiry to about one hundred of these sources.

"But despite our best efforts, we really didn't have any corporate leaders on our board," Hasson remembers. "The board represented the full spectrum of the community, and there was no way that every board member could give $2,500 a year, as they do on big-league boards. Yet, we were in the right place at the right time. Our project was perfect for corporate fundraising. AIDS had been in the headlines for years, but few corporations had done anything. We had a tangible goal—a building—which seemed safe and easy to understand."

Importance of names

Betsy Lieberman agrees but remembers that when it came down to brass tacks, what potential funders looked at were two things: the organization's letterhead, to see who was on the board; and the list of who else gave money. As those lists grew, the fundraising task got easier. "Relating to funders is a bit like relating to in-laws," Lieberman says. "You need to find a way to approach them harmoniously, to know them well enough so you can pull their heartstrings."

All the painstaking proposal writing paid off in fall 1988, when HRSA announced a $500,000 federal grant to the project, with the possibility of more federal money earmarked for the day health program. This public money served as the "lead gift" usually required for a capital campaign.

Now the project could be publicized. A public relations firm volunteered its help. Publicity materials were simple, but professionally designed. Newsletters kept donors abreast of news, but on no regular schedule.

Campaign leadership

The board formed a capital campaign committee, with Hasson as staff and member, and board members Judi Beck (a public relations specialist and mother from a nearby neighborhood), Donald Chamberlain (the tireless board president), Ellen Ferguson (who had extensive fundraising experience), KIRO-TV reporter Micki Flowers, Shirley Bridge, and Patricia McInturff (who oversaw the county's AIDS program). They asked Luke Helms, president of Seafirst Bank, to cochair the campaign with Shirley Bridge; Thatcher Bailey, publisher of Bay Press; and Paul Schell, former director of the city's department of community development and head of Cornerstone Development Corporation. Because of who asked, each agreed.

Ferguson, public relations coordinator for the Burke Museum at the University of Washington, had been involved on other nonprofit boards—but none had raised this kind of money. She chaired the campaign committee as the board began its quest for millions of dollars. Hasson, who had never administered a capital campaign before, brought in veteran fundraiser William Tobin as a consultant. He looked at the traditional formula for capital campaigns— using corporate team leaders—but the needed leaders simply were not there. The senior community leaders were not from the generation most affected by AIDS, and they were afraid of the topic; some had children and grandchildren directly affected, but they preferred not to talk about it. Younger leaders, on the other hand, were not high enough up in corporate hierarchies to bring in the big money.

Lead gifts

In Seattle, many companies look to the Boeing Company as the leader in community giving. Some even joke that their policy is to give a percentage of whatever Boeing gives to capital campaigns. Everybody knew it was going to be important to approach Boeing early. Both Hasson and Lieberman, who were getting good at "the pitch," took board member Gwen Beighle (a minister who directs the Multifaith AIDS Project and is married to a Boeing vice president) to speak with Boeing's corporate director of public and community affairs, Joseph Taller. "We thought the idea had merit," Taller recalls. "And we believe strongly in giving to capital campaigns. We're not a consumer company, we're just trying to be a good corporate citizen" (personal communication, August 12, 1991).

Taller says that Boeing management considered the fact that some neighbors had expressed public opposition to the project, but they decided that the AIDS Housing of Washington project—particularly the adult day-care component—was the "leading edge of a new delivery system. It's cost-effective. And there's a real need out there." In 1989, Boeing gave $200,000, the largest of the Seattle-area corporate and foundation grants received.

Breaking grantmaking ground

This was Boeing's first major grant to an AIDS-related project. Since then, according to directors of social services and arts agencies in the gay and lesbian community, Boeing is less skittish about funding projects emanating from the gay community as well as from other AIDS service organizations.

"The Boeing grant was important for us as a lead grant," says Hasson. "After we had its stamp of approval, it was much easier to get contributions from other local corporations." (In addition, the Boeing Employees Good Neighbor Fund, with a separate decision-making process, gave $90,450 to help furnish Bailey-Boushay House.)

Approaching foundations

Likewise, in the world of private foundations, it was equally important to find a "lead donor." The Seattle Foundation, known to many grant seekers as a stodgy community foundation with little imagination, surprised everyone. Its early $25,000 grant opened doors for other foundations to give. But the grantsmanship game was a long, hard process. When sources turned thumbs down, Hasson or Lieberman would phone the officers in charge and ask if they knew of other possible sources. On more than one occasion, those conversations led to resubmission and eventual grants. Sometimes, AIDS Housing of Washington board members called on friends who sat on foundation boards or staffs to nudge a proposal toward acceptance.

Public-private playoffs

Without question, the mix of public and private money spurred more fence-sitting grantmakers from both worlds to contribute. Private donors saw government money as evidence of the project's likely success; government sources saw private supporters lining up and did not want to say no to what increasingly appeared to be a winning project.

Turning challenges into support

Legal and legislative roadblocks threatened to derail the project, even as fundraising continued. But, in many cases, the challenges to the project served to broaden the base of support and attract media attention.

Visible enemies

As the capital campaign got off the ground, there were other challenges: Neighbors of the selected building site filed a legal challenge to the project, and the legislature almost tabled a special bill that would pay for the additional nursing hours needed to care for people with AIDS. In order to get the private financing to build the residence, the project needed a formal commitment to a higher-level reimbursement for care; that required a special amendment to the state nursing home regulations. After weeks of lobbying by AIDS Housing of Washington staff and planning committee members, the amendment to raise the reimbursement passed in the state assembly unanimously. But the budget committee of the state senate refused to hear the bill. It appeared that all of the planning would go down the drain.

Corporations give more than money

It was not until the corporate lobbyists from Seafirst Bank, Boeing, and Weyerhaeuser got into the act that the logjam broke. These corporations had already decided to fund the project, and people with close connections to them had joined the board. They did not want to see the project fail. The senate budget committee was called into an emergency special session, and the amendment passed in one hour. The bill passed in the state senate unanimously.

Meetings with corporations also yielded important recommendations for board members. Hasson and Lieberman took careful notes on all meetings and telephone conversations with funders and filed the notes for later reference. The board included many people who had never been on boards before, and many board members had not met most of the others before they joined; in that sense, it was truly a broad-based board. Board members often disagreed on the best course of action. But staff and board leadership created a culture where it was all right to disagree. They fostered a sense of mutual respect and made sure board members felt appreciated.

Annual retreats for both staff and board and frequent social events kept spirits up and communication constant. Some staff and board members marched together at the annual gay pride celebration; others walked together at the annual AIDS walk-a-thon, which partially benefited the project.

Staff work vital

"I'm convinced that a good board is important," says Lieberman. "But a board is only as good as the people who staff it. Staff has to make it easy for the board to do its work." At AIDS Housing of Washington, the board and staff were small enough—twenty-five board members, four staff—that a sense of intimacy and trust developed. That dynamic was also infused with a sense of humor. Hasson gave each board member a windup toy: walking, chattering teeth, to remind them to get on the telephone and ask their friends for money after the initial appeal letters were sent. She also gave them refrigerator magnets so that they could keep their "to-call" lists in front of their noses.

Mark Miller, the bookkeeper and office manager, and Jeff Crandall, the administrative assistant, worked as hard and diligently as the most committed volunteer. They frequently put in extra hours to ensure that the details for special events were in place: the name tags, the food and drinks, the literature. All staff had access to board members. Board knew staff. The board formed various committees, each expanded to include nonboard members who wanted to get involved.

Broadening the base of support

With corporate and foundation fundraising well under way, the board turned its attention to individual gifts.

Controversy helped

Vocal opposition by a small number of neighbors helped the project get publicity and support. Newspapers and newsletters across the city editorialized about possible racism, homophobia, and NIMBY-ism (the "not in my backyard" syndrome) among the opponents. The board decided to convene a blue-ribbon advisory board, chaired by visionary business leader James Ellis, to galvanize support and credibility. And Michele Hasson convinced a skeptical staff and board that this was the time for a telemarketing campaign. AIDS Housing of Washington hired a firm that had conducted a successful campaign for the Seattle Art Museum several years before. The campaign's ambitious goal was $800,000. It garnered pledges totaling $941,000.

Telemarketing options and incentives

The week before professional telemarketers solicited potential donors by telephone, letters went to those on a mailing list assembled with help from other AIDS services agencies. Flexibility was a watchword: Donors could pay monthly, quarterly, or every six months, which made it easier for them to stretch to higher levels than their normal giving. High-level gifts were rewarded: $250 with a sweatshirt, $500 with a ticket to the Headdress Ball, and $1,000 with the donor's name permanently engraved on a public artwork in Bailey-Boushay House.

William Block, a lawyer who, in 1990, became the second president of AIDS Housing of Washington, explains, "After all the publicity, all we had to do was ask, and people wanted to be part of the community's response to an urgent need" (personal communication, September 18, 1991). Gay and lesbian groups, church groups, and many individuals sent in checks. Without missing a beat, Hasson was convinced that there were ways to bring in even more people who had not yet become part of that community response. She networked quietly to identify relatives of people who had died of AIDS; many were anxious to contribute once they were located and asked. Likewise, since an arts committee had been meeting to bring the perspective of artists into the building's planning and design, she approached a group of arts patrons who otherwise would not have been likely donors. Because these individuals collected fine art and appreciated its healing qualities, they were interested in ensuring that the AIDS residence contained excellent art. The "niche" project was born. Local artists were commissioned to create works for niches in rooms and hallways; donors paid $1,000 for each niche. Eventually, even one of the project's biggest opponents quietly sent a check.

Endless asking

During the entire campaign, board members held "home parties" where they asked their friends and acquaintances to contribute. At these parties, board members explained why they were involved, and Hasson or Lieberman would give the proverbial "pitch," carefully adapted for each audience. Some board members organized dinners at restaurants; others cooked gourmet dinners in their homes. "It was important to find the comfort level of each board member, because they were all different," Hasson explains. Some got carried away with enthusiasm as the fundraising momentum increased. One, who initially said she would never raise money, ended up writing eighty letters to friends, designating all of her company's United

Way gifts to the project and getting a foundation whose board she sat on to match its board members' gifts.

Naming gifts

Another board member, Thatcher Bailey, whose life partner Frank Boushay had died of AIDS in 1989, raised more money than any other. He spoke passionately of how AIDS had affected his life and of the need for individuals, particularly gay men who had high disposable incomes, to step to the plate for this one-time project. He urged them to furnish a room for $2,500, pay for a bedroom at $25,000, a greenhouse or solarium at $50,000, or a "naming gift" of $250,000. Since no one gave the naming gift, the board decided to name the facility after Bailey and Boushay. "We liked that even better than giving it the name of someone who didn't really work on the project," Ellen Ferguson remembers (personal communication, September 18, 1991).

Special events

People kept bringing special events ideas to the staff: benefit performances, costume balls, art shows, designer showhouses. "If I had it to do again, I'd do fewer special events," Lieberman acknowledges. "They were great for publicity, but many of them took a lot of staff energy and seldom brought in much money. If others want to do them *for* you, fine." In time, the staff learned to say no to high-cost events, and to low-quality equipment donations. But they ensured that a range of events—from the $5 comedy night at Timberline Tavern to the $250 Headdress Ball—allowed people from all income levels to get involved.

Board rewards

Board members and volunteers were rewarded with regular parties (sometimes work parties), glass paperweights, and mentions in the commemorative program, issued at the community dedication in January 1992. The program, which was printed by the Boeing Company, was also condensed and distributed as a twelve-page advertising insert in the daily newspapers to over 147,000 households, extending the reach of the project, and its information about AIDS, even further. A coupon invited, and garnered, further gifts.

Thanks

All of the project's six thousand donors were acknowledged by name in the commemorative program. Each had received a handwritten thank-you card from at least one member of the board or staff. The mailing list was not released to any other groups, since some donors said they did not want their gifts to trigger a flood of new mailed appeals. At the end of the campaign, as Bailey-Boushay House admitted its first residents in 1992, donors were asked whether they wanted to remain on the mailing list to receive news of the facility's programs and progress.

Even after the thirty-four-thousand-square-foot house was completed, people still wanted to help. Hasson was ready: She put a "giving tree" in a prominent spot in the new residence. People who came to tour the facility could sign up to give more money to plant trees or buy videocassette recorders, microwave ovens, or other appliances; their pledges were hung on tags on the branches of the giving tree. After AIDS Housing of Washington scaled back its operation, Hasson was hired by Virginia Mason Medical Center, the new operator of Bailey-Boushay House, to continue in her fundraising role. Now, she faces the world of operating and special project grants, deferred giving, and endowments.

Fundraising principles

Bailey-Boushay House had a lot going for it. The building of the residence was a concrete response to a devastating health crisis; people could see where their money was going and wanted to be part of it. Besides being the "right project at the right time," the Bailey-Boushay experience demonstrates other principles of successful fundraising:

See it as a long-term process. Do not expect instant success.

Build relationships and coalitions across traditional boundaries. Try to find ways for "other types of people" to help.

Ensure that the right people do the asking. And give the askers the tools to do it right: the pitch, the information, the incentives, and the rewards.

Take time to get the right people involved; especially in a controversial project, find well-known mainstream supporters willing to lend their names. Give them the tools to support the project effectively in informal conversations.

State the organization's mission clearly and stick to it; do not make service decisions based on availability of grant dollars; otherwise the mission continually changes.

Figure out how to market what the project "owns"; find the programs that people like and remarket them. Operating money is not sexy.

Do not be afraid to put money into a full-time fund developer. In the end, Bailey-Boushay's fundraising costs totaled only 3.4 percent of the budget.

Try to include start-up costs in a capital campaign. Bailey-Boushay failed to do this, and it almost delayed the facility's opening. The campaign goal kept inflating.

Ensure that the executive director likes fundraising. Her or his leadership is critical.

Take time to nurture and support board members. Insist on 100 percent board giving, even if it is only $10. Challenge them to challenge their friends, but give them the tools to do it.

Create materials that are clear and simple, "nice but not too nice."

Keep in touch by regular communication with donors and careful use of the media.

Do not be afraid to ask for in-kind donations of silverware, furniture, and so on. Many companies will give discounts; some make outright gifts.

Know when to accept benefits, gifts, labor, and in-kind services—and when to say "no, thank you."

Use public support to attract private dollars, and vice versa.

Conclusion

In an era when all too many community action projects aim to block construction of intrusive developments, Seattle citizens point proudly to the AIDS house that they built in response to a critical need. Board member Maria Gonzalez, who supervises construction projects for a living, summed up the personal commitment many of the thousands who contributed to Bailey-Boushay felt: "It was a grieving process . . . taking my grief out of myself and putting it into the community" (personal communication, September 11, 1991).

STEPHEN SILHA *is a Seattle-based freelance writer and communications consultant who has worked for newspapers, foundations, governments, corporations, and nonprofits. He is a board member of AIDS Housing of Washington.*

In 1977, four volunteers started a new organization to care for terminally ill patients. Today, Horizon Hospice is an established institution with an annual operating budget of $2.7 million and an endowment of $730,000, and it is about to launch its first capital campaign. It is the kind of well-managed nonprofit organization with diversified fundraising that makes a better society for all of us.

7

Horizon Hospice: From zero to $2.7 million a year

Joan Flanagan

HOSPICE IS A SPECIAL PROGRAM of care for patients who are dying. American hospices began as part of a reform movement to overcome society's denial of the existence of dying patients. The first hospice programs developed palliative care as an effective treatment option, and then they helped to change public policy toward provision of federal funding for hospice care.

This is a common pattern for improving the quality of life in the United States. Leaders of nonprofit organizations improve our society, first, as outside reformers, then as creators of better models of care and as advocates for mainstream funding, and, finally, as managers of the best programs. Each step is necessary, and each step works because of a diversified funding base that permits the organizations to survive, grow, and flourish.

NEW DIRECTIONS FOR PHILANTHROPIC FUNDRAISING, NO. 1, FALL 1993 © JOSSEY-BASS PUBLISHERS

In the last two years, I have trained 250 fledgling nonprofit organizations in the Czech Republic, Slovakia, Hungary, Poland, and Russia for the Third Sector Project of the Institute for Policy Studies at Johns Hopkins University. Since the Communist regimes in these countries had suppressed democracy and all nonprofit organizations for decades, the contrast with the United States was glaring. It was painfully obvious what citizens are missing when they lack nonprofit groups to create the programs they want or to fight the evils they do not want. The deficiencies were especially blatant in health care. In the former Communist countries, there were no ramps for wheelchairs or braille signs in elevators because there were no organizations of disabled people to lobby for equal access. There were no "no-smoking" areas in public buildings because there were no cancer or heart or lung associations to fight the tobacco industry. It is clear that if any society has to wait for the government alone to create better programs, it will wait forever. On the other hand, we can see in the development of hospice how nonprofit organizations enable citizens in a democracy to create better communities.

Hospice programs have shown that as concerned citizens we can take an old idea of compassionate care of the sickest patients, improve it with the best medical know-how, and create a better form of health care to improve the lives of our families and the budget of our nation. This is the kind of role that American nonprofit organizations, supported by generous citizens and smart grantmakers, can offer as a good example to the rest of the world.

The Horizon Hospice fundraising model

In 1977, four volunteers decided to start the first hospice program in Chicago. They had read of the values of this new form of caring for dying people: Hospice care enables patients to stay pain-free and alert, enables doctors and nurses to admit the prognosis and give effective palliative care, and enables families and friends to play a larger role in caring for the patients. All four volunteers had experience with seriously ill people: Dr. Frank Duda is a pediatrician, Sharon King was the administrator of the pulmonary department at Cook County Hospital, Ada Addington volunteered in the burn unit at Cook County Hospital, and the Reverend J. Wilson Reed is an Episcopal priest. None had ever started a nonprofit organization.

Step by step the number of volunteers, staff, and patients grew, sometimes slowly, sometimes very quickly. In 1993, a team of 42 skilled staff and 131 trained volunteers will care for 360 patients. Fifty-eight percent of the patients have cancer, 37 percent have AIDS, and 5 percent have other diseases. Patients are cared for by their own family or friends, a pair of volunteers, and a staff of professionals. Sixty percent of the patients have chosen to die at home (the national average is 20 percent). The rest of the patients have chosen to die in special units at affiliated health facilities.

State-of-the-art palliative health care has become very expensive. In 1979, Horizon Hospice's entire annual budget was $18,000. In April 1992, Horizon spent $11,000 just on medications, just for one month.

Lessons on fundraising development

Horizon Hospice can serve as a model for fundraising development for any group of people who want to transform a good idea into a permanent effective organization. Although it began with just four volunteers, no paid staff, and no funding, Horizon Hospice has grown into a model health care institution (see Table 7.1). In 1992, 47 percent of the $2 million budget came from reimbursement from Medicare (for patients over sixty-five years of age), 10 percent from Medicaid (for indigent patients), 23 percent from private insurance, and 20 percent came from fundraising. The portion raised from contributions breaks down to 39 percent from individual donors, 24 percent from foundations and trusts, 9 percent from corporations, 5 percent from patient memorials (gifts given in memory of Horizon Hospice patients who died), 4 percent from Saint Joseph's

Table 7.1. Growth of Horizon Hospice, 1977–1993

Year	Volunteers	Patients	Staff	Expenditures	Fundraising Firsts
1977	4	0	0	0	In-kind contributions
1978	8	2	1ᵃ	$306	Cash contributions
1979	35	21	2	$18,000	Patient memorial gifts Foundation grant Executive director Corporate contributions
1980	40	50	2	$48,000	Holiday mailing
1981	50	47	3	$59,000	Musical event
1982	50	60	3	$96,000	Bequest
1983	55	60	4	$103,000	
1984	80	71	4	$168,000	Endowment
1985	100	96	4	$178,000	
1986	78	122	5	$190,000	
1987	105	113	5	$188,000	
1988	139	139	8	$538,000	Gala dinner-dance Medicare reimbursement Finance director Computerized donor base
1989	122	152	12	$767,000	
1990	131	179	16	$1,145,000	
1991	122	227	22	$1,572,000	Director of development United Way priority grant
1992	131	291	30	$2,000,000	Feasibility study
1993	131	360	42	$2,700,000	

a. Single staff member at quarter-time.

Hospice, 3 percent from the interest on endowment, 3 percent from the Chicago Department of Health, and 1 percent from United Way.

Besides being an excellent model, Horizon is also the hospice that I know best. I was recruited for the Horizon Hospice planning committee in 1978, volunteered on the board of directors from 1979 to 1990, and have served on the community advisory board since 1991.

The Horizon fundraising history illustrates two primary fundraising principles:

Independence comes from diversity.

Anything is possible.

Even if an organization is very small, it can grow if the program delivers quality services and the leaders develop a diversified fundraising plan.

There are four factors that have made Horizon Hospice's fundraising program a success. Any group of people can duplicate these success factors to create a self-sufficient organization that raises money in ways that are consonant with the organization's values.

Success factor 1: People

Horizon Hospice founder Ada Addington believes that success comes from choosing people with the ability to follow through in their work. For more than a year, a team of volunteers met every Tuesday evening to discuss the idea of a hospice for Chicago, to learn more about the concept, and to create a tax-exempt nonprofit corporation. Every person did what he or she promised to do, whether it was file forms with the IRS or bring the lemon bars for refreshments. Because there were nine dependable people working, we were able to accelerate the learning curve.

Addington says that every board needs three things: brains, brawn, and bucks. When we started, we had the brawn, several eager workers, but no brains, very little knowledge about hospice care. Fortunately, we were humble enough to know that we needed to learn almost everything, and experienced enough to know that we did not need to reinvent the wheel. Since there were no hospices operating in Illinois, the volunteers spent their own time and money to visit pioneer American hospices in California, Connecticut, Florida, Minnesota, and Wisconsin. Six volunteers took a one-day training course at Royal Victoria Hospital in Montreal, Canada, and six journeyed to London, England, the Mecca of hospice care, to see Saint Joseph's and Saint Christopher's hospices.

The next step was to recruit the brains. Addington recruited the best and the brightest to serve on three advisory boards: medical, business, and community. These gave Horizon Hospice the credibility it needed as a new and controversial program, especially with funders.

The medical advisory board gave the first doctor and nurse access to seven of the best doctors in the city for specialized advice. By recruiting top doctors from six major hospitals, it also gave the tiny program instant legitimacy in the very political world of health care.

The business advisory board gave the officers access to four of the most successful businessmen in the world. After giving advice to the White House, Switzerland, or China, these men would sit down and help Horizon Hospice grow. They were never patronizing, but they always challenged the officers to think bigger and farther. When we were still planning from Tuesday to Tuesday, the business leaders said, "Where's your five-year plan?" When the fundraising team tried resting on their laurels once the annual fund was well established, the business advisers said, "Where's your endowment? You need an income stream for everything that is too controversial to be funded by traditional sources." Gloria Steinem once said, "Rich people plan for the next two generations, poor people plan for Saturday night" (Austin, 1987). It is easier and safer to plan from Tuesday to Tuesday. The business advisers challenged the fundraisers to think bigger and bolder every year.

The community advisory board, composed of writers, architects, broadcast journalists, and funeral home directors, among others, gave advice and specialized expertise as needed. The names of the community leader also provided extra endorsements for funders.

All three advisory boards continue today. They give Horizon Hospice access to some of the wisest people in Chicago, and they give the experts an easy way to share their expertise, even when they lack the time or interest to serve on the board of directors.

Success factor 2: Plan

Once Horizon Hospice had a board of directors to serve as the brawn and do the day-to-day work, and the advisory boards to serve as the brains and supervise long-range planning and quality control, it was time to look for the bucks. But before they made the first fundraising call, the volunteers spent months defining what the hospice should be, who it should serve, and how it should work. The planning team set down the vision of what they wanted Horizon Hospice to be. Like Abraham Lincoln, Frank Duda wrote the goals on the back of an envelope, and this precious document still exists in the Horizon Hospice archives. Some of the early goals were the following: Patients come first. Patients will be pain-free and alert. Health care should be patient controlled and patient oriented. And patients will never die alone.

Sharon King, one of the founders of and the pro bono lawyer for Horizon, today works as the philanthropy adviser to the Rockefellers. King says, "The key to planning in the beginning was the balance between the need to have a big vision and approach it in manageable, achievable steps. The rapid growth in both patient care and fundraising worked because every decision was checked against the touchstone vision: that people who are dying should have control over their last days" (personal communication, May 21, 1992). By keeping this vision in front of everyone, the group had the clarity of values needed to pursue many sources of money. The time had come to begin to ask for bucks.

Success factor 3: Progress

The success of the fundraising program was based on doing what was possible at the time, setting bigger goals each year, and being willing to take risks and try new ideas but, at the same time, not going too far out without a net. Horizon Hospice patient care developed step-by-step. The fundraising plan developed as crawl, step, walk, run, race!

CRAWL. In the first year of the all-volunteer planning committee, every volunteer paid all of his or her own expenses and gave whatever donations were needed for meetings (food, beverages, paper), research (travel, postage, telephone calls), and education (books, meetings). The "office" was a card table and a cardboard box in the president's bedroom. A card file of names was built name-by-name over the first year.

In-kind contributions were vital. Howard Sulkin let us use rooms at DePaul University for volunteer training; Margaret Standish at the Playboy Foundation printed the first annual report; twenty-two people gave talent, such as photography by Joseph Barabe, artwork by Mary Ann McBride, and legal work by Ruth Van Dermark.

STEP. Once incorporated as a 501(c)(3) tax-exempt nonprofit corporation, Horizon Hospice could begin to ask for foundation and corporation grants. The Chicago Community Trust gave the first major grant of $35,000 to support the first year of a full-time paid executive director. It also paid for a "real" office: two small rooms in an old office building that looked more like the setting for a V. I. Warshawski mystery than the cutting edge of health care.

The first executive director, Sally Owen-Still, was an experienced social services agency executive. At her previous job, a very effective and worthwhile agency flourished for three years with 90 percent of its budget coming from one six-figure grant. When the grant ran out, the program had to be cut to the quick. As Disraeli said, "There is no education like adversity." Owen-Still learned that a board of directors has to be involved immediately and continually in building a broad base of donors. At her first meeting with the board, she explained that the Chicago Community Trust grant was a nonrenewable resource, and that the board must make a concerted effort to find more foundations, corporations, and individuals to support a permanent organization.

The partnership between Owen-Still and the board of directors worked well because she had excellent management skills. She was very good at presenting a challenge and then allowing the board to devise a strategy to meet the goal. Fundraising was included on every agenda, and every person was presented with a list of the trustees of local foundations, trusts, and corporate giving programs. Although the executive director prepared most of the foundation and corporate proposals, the leaders on the board made the connections with people they knew, or knew of, and went along on most of the fundraising calls.

In addition to foundation and corporate grants, the organization began to tell its story and ask for money from the general public, too. The McDonald's Corporation paid for the first four newsletters that were sent to the one thousand names on the list compiled from meetings, speeches, and telephone inquiries. Every issue included a request for funds, volunteers, and patients. After the first four issues, Horizon Hospice made enough from donations on each newsletter to cover the production costs.

In 1980, Horizon Hospice conducted its first holiday mailing to ask for money. Since the agency's mailing list was so small, the executive director and president asked each member of the board to address envelopes and write personal notes to each person on his or her Christmas or Hanukkah list. The president, Ada Addington, set the standard by personally addressing four hundred letters. The first year, we started too late and had production problems. Nonetheless, the first holiday mailing raised $6,600 and proved that the public believed in Horizon as a cause worth supporting.

WALK. Excellent patient care, smart grantmakers, and good fundraising work produced grants from Commonwealth Edison, Field Foundation, First National Bank, Harris Bank, T. Lloyd Kelly Foundation, Sara Lee Corporation, W. W. Grainger Company, and other local funders. Bolstered by more corporate, foundation, and individual gifts, in 1981 Horizon Hospice decided it was time to do a fundraising event. Since every possible penny went for patient care, the committee designed a no-cost musical event. The unique element of the fundraiser was the celebrities who were the magnets for the event. The executive director had married her piano teacher, composer and musician Thomas Still. This made Ray Still, the world's finest oboe player and first-chair oboe for the Chicago Symphony Orchestra, her father-in-law. Ray and Tom Still offered to play for an afternoon recital and recruit a few more world-class musicians to help out for free. (Okay, not every organization has world-class celebrities that want to help. But every organization can find someone who is a celebrity. For example, the organization of women office workers in Dayton, Ohio, organized a very successful party around the local TV weatherman.)

Once the celebrities were committed, we could be zealous about getting everything else free. Father Reed donated space at Church of Our Saviour, an exquisite Victorian church with Tiffany windows and a terra-cotta interior that made the Mozart, Vivaldi, and Still compositions sound even better. One board member got Kraft to donate white cheese, yellow cheese, and orange cheese; another board member got an Italian family to donate white wine and red wine. Intoxicated by the glorious music, everyone thought they were getting Stilton and champagne. A recent bride had enough clean table-cloths for the parish hall tables; the suburbanites brought flowers from their yards; a doctor lent four chairs for the stage. *Everything* was donated. The first musical event made $2,000; with the addition of advertising in the program and slight price increases (volunteers got free tickets), the profits went up to $8,000 by the third year.

During the next seven years, Horizon Hospice repeated and improved their techniques for making money. The leaders asked for and got more grants from corporations, foundations, and trusts, such as the Chicago Community Trust, GATX, Kemper Charitable Fund, Otho S. A. Sprague Memorial Fund, Lurie Foundation, and other local grantmakers who understood the importance of hospice.

As we captured the names from every audience and inquiry, individual gifts also went up steadily. The executive director organized the fundraising calendar so that the holiday mailing went out in early November; donations went up as the size of the list grew. This is a good example of the value of repeating an effective fundraising technique. Now the board and volunteers know they will be addressing envelopes and writing notes in October; the donors know they will get a request at the holidays and, we hope, will fit Horizon Hospice into their Christmas, Hanukkah, or Kwanzaa giving plans. The timing and format are similar every year, but the list and the amount requested grow each year. The income grew twelvefold from $6,600 to $80,000 from 1980 to 1992.

RUN. When it was only five years old, Horizon Hospice received its first bequest, for $25,000, from the estate of a patient who had been a longtime acquaintance of some of the volunteers. In 1983, the board decided to use this gift as the nucleus for an endowment fund and set a goal of $500,000. Every member of the board of directors gave at least $1,000 to launch the endowment fund, and to establish credibility for the young agency. A separate fundraising committee was created to ask for larger gifts and bequests to the endowment fund in order to establish a dependable income stream for future work.

RACE. In 1987, the board voted to apply for certification to receive Medicare funding. After years of debate, the issue was finally settled by going back to the most fundamental value of the hospice: Patients come first. Therefore, in 1988, Horizon Hospice began receiving Medicare reimbursement for services rendered, and the board of directors committed itself to raising the additional money needed for acceptance of federal funds. Although Medicare and Medicaid funding creates much larger fundraising goals, the board and staff know that this was the right choice because it enables the hospice to serve more people and serve them better.

The decision to accept Medicare funds meant that the hospice could give up to six hours a day of hands-on care to the patients. Medicare covers part of the costs for caring for a hospice patient: nurses, doctors, home health aides, medicines, and medical equipment. The response of families has been very positive. It is especially good for the poorest patients, because the public funds and private fundraising pay for all of their care, medications, and equipment.

The fundraising challenge comes in three forms: The federal government only pays part of the costs, it pays very slowly, and it does not pay for all services. For example, in 1992, it cost an average of

$138 per patient per day for care. The average Medicare reimbursement was $95 per day. So the staff, board, and volunteers needed to raise $43 per patient per day to pay for the gap between real costs and reimbursement.

The second problem with Medicare and Medicaid funding is that even with the best administrative staff and state-of-the-art computers and software, the time between expenditure and reimbursement averages 120 days. The state of Illinois has been as much as seven months late on reimbursements. To cover the cash-flow lag, Horizon Hospice spends about $240,000 every year. In other words, we need to increase our fundraising goal by $240,000 to cover the costs until we are reimbursed. (For costs to draw even with reimbursements, Horizon would have to go out of business; seven months later the books would zero out.)

The third fundraising challenge created by government funding is that it does not pay for all of the services that the hospice wants to provide. One hospice principle is that "dying is a family affair." The family and friends caring for the dying patient are also given care, including bereavement care for at least a year after the death of the patient. In addition to providing for the physical and emotional needs of patient families, hospice also helps them care for their spiritual needs. Medicare funding does not pay for either bereavement services or spiritual care, so these and other nonreimbursable expenses must be covered out of dollars raised from private sources.

In Illinois, "the land of Lincoln," we believe in "government of the people, by the people, and for the people." We *are* the government, and those of us who can must provide for those of us who cannot—in this case, through our tax dollars. However, although we are idealistic enough to believe that some public funds should be allocated to people who are most ill, we are also realistic enough to know that use of tax dollars dramatically increases the fundraising goals that hospice leaders must raise from individuals, corporations, and foundations.

At Horizon, a finance director was hired to work full-time, billing third-party payers, negotiating agreements, and keeping track of the zillions of details created by accountability for private and public funds. While attention to detail and good fiscal management are desirable standards anyway, the quantity of paperwork generated is a necessary burden to guarantee proper use of public dollars. The addition of a computer expert enabled the hospice to transfer thousands of donor names from handwritten three-by-five-inch cards to a computerized donor base in 1988.

As the fundraising program continued to grow, it finally became evident that too many aspects of the program were not getting the kind of follow-through needed to maintain and increase funding. Even the best board and staff need someone to serve as "mission control," to challenge the leaders to ask for new and larger gifts, to organize the fundraising strategy and calendar, and to keep the program focused. So, in 1991, Horizon Hospice hired its first full-time director of development to work with the executive director and the board of directors.

One advantage of success is that an organization can take on larger, more complicated projects with more partners. Although not a United Way agency, Horizon Hospice received almost $300,000 in 1991 in a United Way priority grant to coordinate four agencies working with people with AIDS. This and other high-quality work done for AIDS patients positioned Horizon Hospice to receive part of the profits of the hugely successful benefit organized by the Design Industries Foundation for AIDS. These and other new funders have joined the base of loyal foundations, corporations, and individuals that have supported Horizon's work over the years.

Success factor 4: Persistence

Persistence is the key to success in fundraising. There have always been problems facing hospice fundraisers, and there always will be problems. A commitment to the values and visions of their organizations can give fundraisers the strength to persevere.

Hospice is not an easy sell. Most people do not want to talk about death and dying. Many people have phobias about cancer, and some people have prejudices against people with AIDS. It is hard to get donations, and even harder to get volunteers. Compared to other causes, hospice fundraisers have to ask more people more often for help.

Unlike the symphony or the opera, hospice has no status symbols or social cachet to offer. Fundraisers cannot offer champagne in the green room with the prima donna or box seats to hear the sold-out superstar. Unlike direct-action community organizing projects, there is no "or else." Hospices do not boycott, picket, or protest the funders who turn them down. Since fundraisers cannot engage in either positive social rewards or negative retaliation, money comes in only because of hard work for a good cause.

Thomas West, physician and medical director of Saint Christopher's Hospice in London, England, said this of hospice care: "It takes courage to go and talk to someone who you know is dying. It takes more courage to let them talk to you. It takes more courage still to sit in silence and not to fill that silence with idle chatter about the snow. And it takes the most courage of all to go back the next day and the next" (West, 1979, p. 7).

Good fundraisers also know that they have to go back the next day and the next. Especially as Americans face an uncertain economy, reform of the health care system, and increased demand for more expensive services from sicker patients, it will take much more work by many more people to raise the needed funds. If we have the courage of our convictions, we also must have the persistence to keep asking for more money from more sources.

What is next for Horizon Hospice's fundraising?

The hospice movement began as a reform movement to provide the most ill and most helpless people in our society effective and humane health care. Now it has grown to be a major player in the health care industry, complete with tax dollars and for-profit entrepreneurs in

competition with the nonprofits. After fifteen years in the trench-
es, we have learned how to focus our anger, direct our energies, and
give our love to the cause of the patients served by hospice. The
same values can drive us over the course of the next fifteen years.

References
Austin, B. "Gloria Steinem." Chicago Tribune, Jan. 11, 1987, p. F3.
West, T. *Hospice: How and Why*. Philadelphia: Episcopal Community Services
Conference, 1979.

JOAN FLANAGAN *is author of* The Grass Roots Fundraising Book
and Successful Fundraising *(Chicago: Contemporary Books). As a professional fundraiser, she trains thousands of the top fundraisers in the United States, Canada, and Europe every year.*

In 1975, rape, child sexual abuse, and domestic violence were viewed as isolated misfortunes. The voice of The Julian Center, a small women's agency in the heartland of America, was rarely heard, and the center's future did not appear promising. Since then, the situation has changed dramatically; by January 1992, the center was thriving financially, growing, and, due to the Tyson rape trial, receiving international media attention.

8

Violence against women: The success of a pioneering effort in the development of services for victims

Naomi Tropp

IN THE MID 1970s, the lives of American women were changing. Tanya Vonnegut Beck was a good example of the evolving social order. She was one of the first women to be ordained as an Episcopal priest. As a frontierswoman, she was particularly aware of the stress created by rapid transition and she wanted to help other women who were experiencing disorder and emotional pain.

Beck asked the bishop of the Episcopal Diocese of Indianapolis to assist her in locating funds to complete a six-month study that would identify the needs of adolescent girls and women. The Lilly Endowment provided a grant for that purpose. At the end of the grant period, Beck returned to the endowment with strong proof

NEW DIRECTIONS FOR PHILANTHROPIC FUNDRAISING, NO. 1, FALL 1993 © JOSSEY-BASS PUBLISHERS

of the need for a human services agency to help the women of central Indiana.

The resulting agency was named The Julian Mission, honoring Julian of Norwich. Julian, who lived in England during medieval times, was one of the first published women authors and a skilled lay counselor, who referred to herself as a "listener." Although the name was changed to The Julian Center in 1981, the agency's services have always reflected Beck's original vision for the mission, that of a place where women's voices would be heard and taken seriously. She wrote, "The Mission would foster an open, confronting, active listening approach in dealing with the crisis situations in women's lives, offering immediate care and concern."

Defining direction: Agency mission

The Julian Center's original mission statement addressed the goals of meeting the emotional, physical, and spiritual needs of women. These broad and lofty goals were to be met with a tiny staff and very limited resources. In its early days, attempting to be all things to all women, the agency provided everything from assertiveness classes to financial planning workshops. However, from the day the center opened its doors in July 1975, the staff received clear and unexpected signals that identified the most urgent, unmet needs of the women in central Indiana. A seemingly endless number of women recounted horrifying tales of rape, child sexual abuse, and domestic violence. In response, the agency developed services to meet the needs of victims of abuse and assault. Between 1975 and 1981, the center grew slowly and expanded these special services. There were no other local agencies concentrating on violence against women, and agency staff started to be viewed as experts in this area.

In 1982, the center more than doubled in size when it opened Sojourner, its shelter for battered women and their children. This shelter was then and remains today the only program of its kind in the eight-county central Indiana area. With the addition of the shelter, the agency was clearly moving in new directions. Now, a significant portion of its client population consisted of victims of violence.

Despite this shift in the center's path, the original mission statement was still intact in 1983, when I was hired as the executive director of the agency. At that time, the center was experiencing a serious financial crisis, and there was some question as to whether the agency would survive. Faced with a $200,000 deficit, no emergency funding in sight, and a disorganized and dispirited staff and board, it became apparent that the time had come to review the organization's mission and goals.

Although the center had drifted toward specializing in violence-against-women issues, the movement had not been planned. Not only was the mission statement outdated, but so too were the agency's printed materials. In essence, the community was being told that the agency was teaching women to handle their finances and deal with dual-career families, when in fact these services were on the decline. On the other hand, abuse and assault issues, which were becoming the mainstay of agency programs, were rarely mentioned. There was, evidently, fear that these issues would be considered controversial and that public discussion of them would endanger the agency's financial security. The opposite turned out to be the case.

By the mid 1980s, the center had deliberately narrowed its focus and, finally, taken charge of its course. The mission statement was completely revised to reflect the agency's commitment to working with women who were victims of violence or experiencing other serious emotional crises. All education programs and support groups that did not reflect the new mission were dropped. New printed materials, such as brochures and annual reports, were created. All of the agency's energies were focused primarily on women and interpersonal violence.

The agency, finally, had a clear focus that dealt with urgent issues, and the community began to respond positively to its message. The center had learned the hard way that a vision that has meaning to both the agency and the community it serves must exist before funders and volunteers will make a commitment to ensure that the organization survives. This definition of direction was, undoubtedly, the most important and difficult obstacle that the agency had to overcome on its route toward maturity.

This problem of defining the agency's mission was not simply a matter of narrowing the focus and planning for the future but rather of uncovering a cardinal truth: If the issues that an organization deems most urgent are controversial, one cannot hide them in the shadows. To hide them is to lose the soul of the work. What one must do, with all of the skill and passion that can be mustered, is convince the community that the issues are directly related to its health and welfare.

At the base: Start-up funds

From July 1975 to the present, each new division of the center has been initially well funded through foundation grants. It is unlikely that the agency would have survived without procuring a solid, albeit temporary, base for its fledgling programs, as those funders who provide ongoing dollars are rarely willing to distribute funds to organizations that have not proved both the need for and the effectiveness of their services. The Julian Center was fortunate that the Lilly Endowment understood the importance of the development of a special agency for women. The endowment provided several years of funding for both of the agency's primary divisions, the counseling center and the battered women's shelter. While the Lilly funds kept shelter operations going, funds from the Indianapolis Foundation made renovation of the building possible. By the time each of these grants had run its course, there was proof that the programs were being well used and that it was in the community's best interest to continue to have them available for the many women who needed them.

The Health Foundation of Greater Indianapolis, recognizing the need for nonprofit organizations to cultivate those skills that facilitate successful fundraising, also provided the center with a three-year grant. These funds were used to hire and train a development director, create an agency videotape and other promotional materials, and purchase computer equipment.

The agency plans to continue to procure foundation grants to create pilot projects. Such funding allows for responsible experimentation that can lead to possible solutions to difficult social problems.

Meat and potatoes: Sources of ongoing funds

Most nonprofit organizations depend on several key sources for a portion of their ongoing annual revenues. Although government cutbacks and fluctuations in the success of United Way campaigns have led us to understand that nothing is permanent, certain types of funds can still be viewed as ongoing, despite their ebbs and flows. The Julian Center has been more fortunate than many agencies in that United Way has funded approximately 50 percent of its budget over the last fourteen years, and federal and state funds have provided a significant portion of the shelter's budget since its inception.

Other than proving that there is a need for the services rendered and that they are well provided and managed, the agency's success in procuring and maintaining these funds relates directly to its willingness to spend the time to meet the needs of the funders and to develop meaningful professional relationships with government staff and United Way staff and volunteers. There is no doubt that organizations and institutions that provide ongoing funding require lots of reports, audits, program evaluations, and meetings. It has been The Julian Center's experience that just as it is worthwhile for an individual to work hard to earn his or her meat and potatoes, it is worthwhile for nonprofit agencies to work hard to earn theirs.

On our own: Special events and projects

There was a time when some nonprofits received all of their funding from "permanent" sources. They were not responsible for going out into the community to raise their own funds. With few exceptions, those days are long gone. Start-up grants come to an end, and ongoing funds rarely come close to covering current expences, much less to providing for expansion. One of the respones to this dilemma has always been to operate special events. The Julian Center has come a long way in terms of its expertise and success in this arena.

The development and implementation of the center's early events were almost completely dependent on the time, energy, and skill of volunteers. Themes were directly related to the agency's mission and marketed to a narrow segment of the population. The best example of this type of project was Renaissance Woman, which celebrated local women in the arts. Those attending were treated to many different types of displays and performances. They enjoyed the experience. However, the event was expensive to operate and ticket prices were, of necessity, high. Only a small portion of the local community was both interested in the program and able to afford to attend. Profits were negligible.

In the early 1980s, the distinct lack of success of early efforts sent an explicit message to the staff and board members, who did not want history to repeat itself. It was decided that the center needed a sizable annual fundraising event that would appeal to the largest possible audience. We determined that the theme of the project need not be connected, even loosely, to the agency's mission. It did have to be an idea that would have longevity, as its purpose would be to raise substantial amounts of money year after year.

We had learned our lessons well! The resulting event, the Amish Country Market, is now into its eighth year and continues to grow. This old-fashioned country fair, with an Amish theme, pulls in well over ten thousand persons on one Saturday, late in August, each year, and 1992 net profits were over $80,000. When planning the first market, the agency took advantage of an increasing interest in both the Amish people and country crafts, foods, and antiques. The event appeals to people of all ages and many backgrounds. The gate fee has been kept low so that individuals and families with widely varying income levels can afford to attend. People come for many reasons. Some are avid buyers, others enjoy the festive atmosphere, and still others bring small children, who delight in the buggy rides and petting zoo. Most of these folks would attend the market regardless of whom it benefited. Although information on The Julian Center is provided to everyone coming through the gates, the event's primary purpose remains fundraising rather than educating the public about the center's issues and services.

Each year, those who plan the event work hard to make improvements and add new attractions, such as the country music concert and live auction that were new to the market in 1992. Marketing strategies have grown to include mention in national publications such as *Country Living*, and a growing number of people now travel from as far away as Florida and California to attend the event. In other words, despite the achievements of the event, the agency has learned not to rest on its laurels but to do whatever is necessary to ensure continued success.

Another element that is crucial to the health of the Amish Country Market is the use of over three hundred volunteers on the day of the event. The agency had learned difficult lessons in this area as well. Unlike those paying to attend, volunteers are concerned about the center's issues and willing to offer their time and energy to keep the agency afloat. This does not mean, however, that they will automatically come back annually. During much earlier fundraising efforts, volunteers were not provided with sufficient staff support, often overloaded with burdensome tasks, and not always thanked properly for their help. Needless to say, many of these persons did not come back for more.

Today's volunteers are offered a wide variety of positions, reasonable workloads, and lots of support (including free cold drinks and special parking privileges), and they are thanked and thanked and thanked for their help. They each receive a report that lets them know the outcome of the event, so that they fully understand the impact of their assistance. They are considered friends and treated as such. They come back year after year.

We have also attempted, as much as humanly possible, to make the process of raising funds enjoyable for our volunteers. Too frequently, fund development is viewed as a necessary evil and approached with dread. Creativity, comradery, and laughter should simply be made part of this type of collaboration.

Once the agency understood why a fundraising project succeeded, the creation of new events became a welcome, rather than a dreaded, challenge. In 1991, the center cosponsored a concert that sold out, and we plan to repeat that success each year. Selling a product had never been seriously considered, but one was found that was so appealing that, in 1992, the agency embarked on a new adventure: We established a marketing program for the sale of "house pins," wearable art created to assist organizations providing services to homeless populations. Additional ideas are being explored, each of them innovative and sure to excite a community grown weary of overused fundraising concepts. Each new achievement energizes the center's staff and board and leads to the next.

Building a family: Creating links with the community

Shortly before we hired a development director and revamped our fundraising program, I met with a veteran professional fundraiser, anxious to take advantage of his wisdom. At that time, The Julian Center was just crawling out of the financial hole that almost destroyed it, and the achievement of real prosperity still seemed like a distant dream. Of course, I would have loved to have been told that there were keys to unlock the mystery of success and then to have been handed those keys on a red-velvet pillow. Instead, he told me that there were no secrets. He advised that being an outstanding fundraiser had less to do with being clever than with being steady and patient and knowing how to build warm, long-term relationships with a wide variety of individuals, organizations, and corporations. He told me that it took years for these slow, steady efforts to pay off, but that the payoff was well worth the wait. Thank goodness I believed him!

The center did not have to start from scratch. The Episcopal Diocese of Indianapolis founded the agency and continued to support it with those funds that they could afford and with ongoing emotional support. They were always a rock to cling to when the storm got rough. Despite substantial troubles, there were a few individuals and groups that recognized how important the center's survival was to the community and stuck with it through the hard times. They were a small but committed group of friends, and the work of maintaining these relationships, while building new ones, was important.

Build new ones we did! It was, indeed, a slow process, requiring many meetings and speaking engagements and correspondence and yet more meetings. The process was different for each individual or group, just as it is with each friendship built in one's private life. The outcome has been extraordinary. The number of individual donors has grown annually. Many of them are previous clients, and the center could experience no greater tribute than to have their ongoing financial support. Two wonderful sisters created a fund that assists women as they leave the battered women's shelter and attempt to create new and safer lives for themselves and their children. This type of support, whether it comes in the form of a five-dollar check or a multithousand-dollar fund, continuously reminds us that the community cares about our work and believes that we are doing it well, and the support inspires us to do more.

Relationships with women's organizations have proved remarkably fruitful. Many of these organizations raise funds annually and provide funds to different agencies each year. Their efforts are applauded, and the center is always delighted when chosen as a recipient. However, the relationships that have truly sustained the agency and enabled continued growth have been with the growing number of groups who have adopted the center as their special cause and continue to support it year after year. Soroptomists, for example, have been providing the center with significant funds for many years, and one of their past presidents now serves as a member of our board of directors. These groups do not ask that the agency assist with their fundraising efforts. Their members do the work and the center enjoys the profits.

Indy Runners sponsors an annual walk-run for women; that group decided in 1990 to start contributing the proceeds to the center. They have been successful in attracting corporate sponsors for the event, and, as a result, additional businesses have become aware of the center's work.

The Network of Women in Business created a Julian Center committee that is assisting the agency with a variety of projects, including fundraising. They were the first organization to ask to have a representative act as a nonvoting member of the center's board in order to create a stronger link between the two groups. One of those women became so interested in the agency that she now serves as a voting member of the board. The development of stronger bonds between the center and supportive organizations, by having their members serve as board members, has been one of the most critical outcomes of these valuable relationships.

The task of establishing ongoing relationships with corporations provided a distinct challenge for a variety of reasons. The local United Way does not allow its affiliates to ask local corporations for contributions to support operating budgets. It is, of course, the right of any business to make an independent decision to provide such support, and many do. The Julian Center fully understands United Way's need to protect its own campaign and gladly follows its regulations. We have, however, been able to seek corporate support for our fundraising projects and have been increasingly successful in doing so.

The agency's largest fundraising project, the Amish Country Market, has fixed expenses of close to $20,000 per year. It has been the center's goal for many years to find corporate support to underwrite as many of these expenses as possible. Early efforts were completely unsuccessful, both because the event was not yet a known quantity and, once again, because the time had not been taken to slowly build relationships with local corporations. It is also crucial that a business understand the connection between the particular fundraising event and its customers—in other words, how connecting their name with an event will have a positive impact on their business. As with other aspects of fund development, once we identified the barriers to progress, we were on our way to moving beyond them.

As examples of the rewards reaped, National City Bank designed all of the promotional materials for the Amish Country Market and has printed them for several years at no cost to the agency, and Marsh Supermarkets has provided financial support for the event, free advertising in their supplements in local newspapers, and distribution of promotional materials through their stores all over the state. These partnerships have proved mutually beneficial. The Amish Country Market is viewed as a wholesome, family event. In many ways, it mirrors the values of the population of the Midwest, and these are the same people who may choose to bank with National City Bank or buy their groceries at one of the many stores in the Marsh chain.

As with agency volunteers, the center has done an increasingly effective job of thanking individual, organizational, and corporate donors for their support. We have done so not only because we want to ensure continuation of their assistance but also because we truly appreciate their concern about our issues. The ways in which the center thanks its contributors are not unique. The important thing is doing it and meaning it.

The media and our issues

The Julian Center clearly learned many lessons that led to its eventual prosperity and growth. From clearly defining our mission to learning the steps necessary to create a family of supporters, the agency has developed its own unique path to success and continues to follow it to even better days ahead. However, without the powerful impact of television, radio, newspapers, and magazines, violence-against-women issues may have never reached the prominence they enjoy today, and the center's progress might very well have been at a snail's pace.

The agency is enormously grateful to all of those editors, reporters, and producers who have taken the time to educate themselves about the issues. They have, on the whole, done an outstanding job of bringing these difficult and often controversial problems to the attention of a public that was, as recently as ten years ago, unaware that rape, domestic violence, and child sexual abuse are so prevalent in our society. That said, the center played an important role in bringing these concerns to the attention of the media and has worked with them, year after year, on the increasing amount of coverage of violence against women. We have learned that nonprofit organizations should never assume that media representatives will come to them. Building a relationship with reporters is no different from creating a bond with a funder. They can be as important to an agency's survival as any financial contribution.

The center has also watched carefully for unusual opportunities to work with the media. The best example of our success in this regard is the role that we played during Mike Tyson's rape trial. Months before the trial commenced, we positioned ourselves to assist reporters and to take advantage of an unprecedented opportunity to educate people, all over the world, about sexual assault. We sent memos to local, national, and international media informing them that I would be on-site during the trial to provide them with information about rape and to do interviews. We put together a packet of information about both rape and the center, which I distributed to the reporters covering the trial. We compiled a list of rape victims who were willing to talk to reporters and arranged for a number of interviews. I obtained, after considerable effort, one of the local television station's passes and was able to view the entire trial.

The outcome of the center's effort was spectacular! I was the only expert on sexual assault who viewed the trial and was available to reporters full-time. I provided information behind the scenes in addition to the many interviews I did with television, radio, and newspaper reporters. The center met all of its goals in regard to the trial. We helped ensure that the issue of rape was well covered. We educated many reporters about sexual assault and reached consumers of that reporting all over the world. It is not every day that a relatively small human services agency, in the heartland of America, finds itself in the middle of an international news story. What we learned from this experience is that one never knows when such opportunities will appear, and that they can be used to the advantage of a human services agency if the staff are well organized and assert themselves.

The results of this particular opportunity are still unfolding. The agency has already received additional recognition, volunteers, funds, and clients as a direct result of the role we played during the Tyson trial. We are now much more keenly aware of the many ways in which a nonprofit organization, without financial cost, can disseminate its message.

Looking toward the future

Now into its eighteenth year, The Julian Center's issues are receiving more attention than ever before. At times, it feels as if the agency is in the middle of a television miniseries. The developments over the last few years have been frequent and dramatic. As a result of the Kennedy Smith and Tyson rape trials, people all over the world are talking about sexual assault. Reports of rape are up and more victims are seeking counseling. The Hill-Thomas hearings brought the issue of sexual harassment into prominence, and, since then, reports of such abuse have increased substantially and corporations all over the country are taking steps to alleviate the problem. The center recently started offering support groups for victims of harassment. The sexual assaults at the U.S. Navy's Tailhook convention have led to increased discussion of the ways in which women are treated, not only in the military but throughout our society. The center continues to be offered new opportunities to teach and to heal.

The agency's most important strength has been its flexibility. Trailblazing can be intimidating, but exhilarating, and the more experience an organization has doing it, the more likely it is to be successful. The center's history has been so intense and packed full of adventure that it has been forced to mature rapidly in order to survive. Now that services for victims have been established and are well funded, the center is looking toward the twenty-first century, planning programs that will continue to increase the awareness of and, with perseverance, eventually reduce the incidences of violence against women.

NAOMI TROPP *is executive director of The Julian Center in Indianapolis, Indiana.*

*The eight organizations profiled in this volume offer
important lessons on how to conduct successful fundraising endeavors.*

9

Conclusion

Michael Seltzer

WHAT LESSONS CAN WE DRAW from these accounts of successful
endeavors in such diverse settings as Chicago, Indianapolis, Seattle, Philadelphia, San Antonio, and eastern Tennessee that can inform
nonprofit endeavors everywhere? In reviewing these stories, one is
struck by some common threads. In almost every instance, a "chosen" or "called" leader emerges as the organizational hero—whether
she is Linda Blackaby in Philadelphia, whose drive, vision, and commitment ultimately earned her the governor's prestigious arts award
or he is the late Walter Bremond, who built a black empowerment
movement from the ashes of the Watts riots in 1966. Yet, in eastern
Tennessee, it is also clear that it is not one individual but many who
have built Save Our Cumberland Mountains into a dynamic organization of over fifteen hundred members.

Each story recounts various obstacles that would have discour-
aged less persistent and dedicated souls. Leaders were able to mobilize the financial resources, the human talents, and the political clout
of significant sectors of their respective communities to sustain their
initiatives. In Philadelphia and Seattle, respectively, the Neighborhood Film/Video Project and Bailey-Boushay House anchored their
initiatives through affiliations with larger nonprofit institutions. It

NEW DIRECTIONS FOR PHILANTHROPIC FUNDRAISING, NO. 1, FALL 1993 © JOSSEY-BASS PUBLISHERS

is also clear that a mission served not only as the guidepost but also as the foundation for each effort.

What is also important to note is the significant role of financial angels, such as the Episcopal Diocese of Indiana and the Lilly Endowment (The Julian Center), Boeing (Bailey-Boushay House), the Phelps-Stokes Fund (American Indian College Fund), and the Cummins Engine Corporation (National Black United Fund). These founding supporters provided important financing at critical junctures in the early years of their grantees. In several instances, their grants were quite substantial and ongoing. Herein lies a message for many contemporary grantmakers, who are genuinely seeking to maximize the impact of their limited resources.

Yet, of course, no executive director succeeds without the involvement of many others, and no angel continues to provide all necessary support forever. In each case, staff, board members, and volunteers had to roll up their sleeves and reach out to other monied sources in their communities and target segments of the general public as well. Identification of the most appropriate segments of their potential donor audiences or markets was a challenge that each organization had to address. The American Indian College Fund reached out to its potential donor base through the effective use of media, film, and the arts. The Julian Center was able to recruit new supporters who might not otherwise have been drawn to their work through its sponsorship of the Amish Country Market. The National Black United Fund seized on the workplace as a cost-effective charitable arena to reach African American workers. Bailey-Boushay House was able to conduct a successful citywide campaign, utilizing daily newspapers, direct mail, telemarketing, special events, and face-to-face solicitation. For many, the well-chosen special event served as the initial vehicle to build public support. Save Our Cumberland Mountains in Tennessee was even able to extend its reach to Washington, D.C., where a supporter organizes an annual benefit crabfest and auction.

In turning to the public sector for support, several organizations, such as the Guadalupe Cultural Arts Center, Bailey-Boushay House, and Horizon Hospice, also bring into the spotlight a key question not only for the nonprofit sector but for all of American society in the 1990s and beyond: What is the role of government in ensuring the quality of life of its citizens? As emerging nonprofit leaders around the globe look to their counterparts in the United States for guidance and assistance, this question takes on special significance, especially in the newly reestablished nations of Eastern Europe and the Commonwealth of Independent States. We did not set out to answer this key question in this volume, but it is certainly worthy of future consideration. After all, for example, should adequate housing and medical care for people living with AIDS, not to mention all Americans, be ensured by government, or by private philanthropy?

Where government responsibility for the common good ends and the nonprofit's role begins is a central issue of our time, and it certainly will continue to command much sustained national dialogue among all interested parties in the years ahead. Perhaps an answer lies in stories such as that of Save Our Cumberland Mountains.

The chapters in this volume shed light on different fundraising techniques and strategies. Also, the authors reveal much about how the raising of funds enables organizations to turn visions into realities, and to produce a better society for all.

Every profession needs to take stock of itself regularly to remind its practitioners of its origins. It is highly fitting that the chapters in the inaugural issue of this journal profile eight nonprofit organizations in the United States. Through the authors' recounting of their organizations' fundraising trials and tribulations, we are reminded of why people work in the nonprofit sector and why people raise funds.

MICHAEL SELTZER *is a senior consultant specializing in nonprofit institutions and philanthropy at The Conservation Company, New York City; executive director of Funders Concerned About AIDS; and president of the Nonprofit Management Association.*

Index

Community: and American Indian College Fund, 78–81; and The Julian
Center, 134–137; and Neighborhood Film/Video Project, 10–11
Consultants, 18–19, 36, 48–49
Cummins Engine Foundation,
57–58, 61, 65

Davis, E. B., 15–18, 21
Davis, K. E., 55, 66
Deloria, J., Jr., 75
Domestic violence. *See* The Julian
Center
Donor base, 44–48, 142
Donor relations, 45–46
Douglas, P., 67
Drexel University, 14
Drucker, P. F., 58

Episcopal Diocese of Indianapolis,
127, 135, 142

Film: on American Indians, 90, 91; and
community education, 10–11; for
fundraising, 10–12; Latino, 31; and
progressive social causes, 11–12.
See also Neighborhood Film/Video
Project
Financial angels, 142
Flanagan, J., 41
Folklife Center (Philadelphia), 16, 17,
19, 20
Ford Foundation, 58
Fundraising: arts councils, 25–26, 28,
34–36; and boards of directors, 35,
46, 50–51, 107; consultants, 18–19,
36, 48–49; and delayed gratification, 50; domestic violence center,
132–137; and donor base, 44–48,
142; film projects, 11–14; films as,
mechanism, 10; and fulfilling
dreams, 3–4; and fun, 50; goal setting, 49; grass-roots organization,
40–51; health care organization,
99–109, 112–124; higher education
organization, 86–89; lessons/princi-
ples, 47–51, 108–109, 115–124; and
mutual respect, 50; payroll deduction, 63–65; and power distribution, 49–50; and private employer
campaigns, 67–68; and revenue

diversity, 47–48; social change
organization, 63–68; statistics for
U.S., 4, 53; and suspension of disbelief, 50; training, 41. *See also*
Donor base; Grants

Georgakas, D., 13
Grants: American Indian College Fund,
83; Bailey-Boushay House, 102;
Guadalupe Cultural Arts Center,
35; Horizon Hospice program,
118–119; Neighborhood
Film/Video Project, 11–14
Gray, S. T., 49, 68
Griffin, B., 61
Guadalupe Cultural Arts Center
(GCAC) (San Antonio, Tex.):
board of directors, 30–31; director,
29–30; funding, 24–26, 28;
fundraising efforts, 34–36; and
Latino artistic tradition/organiza-
tions, 24–25, 33–34; and Latino
political power, 24–25; management control issues, 28–29; mission, 32–34; organizational scope,
31–32; precursor organization,
25–26; professional management,
26–27, 29–30; revenue sources, 32,
35; Tejano Conjunto Festival, 27,
31–32

Health care. *See* Bailey-Boushay House;
Horizon Hospice program
Health Foundation of Greater
Indianapolis, 130
Higher education. *See* American Indian
College Fund
Hodgkinson, V. A., 53
Horizon Hospice program (Chicago):
advisory boards, 115–116; bequests,
121; crawl/step/walk/run/race
fundraising plan, 117–123; director,
118–119; expenses, 113; fundraising model, 112–113; future,
124–125; grants, 118–119;
Medicare funding, 114, 121–122;
as model health care organization,
113–114; people factor, 115–116;
persistence factor, 123–124; planning factor, 116–117; progress factor, 117–123; revenues, 113–114;

Ordering Information

NEW DIRECTIONS FOR PHILANTHROPIC FUNDRAISING is published quarterly in Fall, Winter, Spring, and Summer and available for purchase by subscription and individually.

SUBSCRIPTIONS for 1993–94 cost $59.00 for individuals (a savings of 35 percent over single-copy prices) and $79.00 for institutions, agencies, and libraries. Please do not send institutional checks for personal subscriptions. Standing orders are accepted.

SINGLE COPIES cost $19.95 when payment accompanies order. (California, New Jersey, New York, and Washington, D.C., residents please include appropriate sales tax.) Billed orders will be charged postage and handling.

DISCOUNTS for quantity orders are available. Please write to the address below for information.

ALL ORDERS must include either the name of an individual or an official purchase order number. Please submit your order as follows:
Subscriptions: specify series and year subscription is to begin
Single copies: include individual title code (such as PF1)

MAIL ALL ORDERS TO:
Jossey-Bass Publishers
350 Sansome Street
San Francisco, California 94104-1310

FOR SINGLE-COPY SALES OUTSIDE OF THE UNITED STATES CONTACT:
Maxwell Macmillan International Publishing Group
866 Third Avenue
New York, New York 10022-6221

FOR SUBSCRIPTION SALES OUTSIDE OF THE UNITED STATES, contact any international subscription agency or Jossey-Bass directly.